YOUNG MATHEMATICIANS AT
Constructing Number Sense, Addition, and

Fostering Children's
Mathematical Development,
Grades PreK–3

The Landscape of Learning

YOUNG MATHEMATICIANS AT WORK
Constructing Number Sense, Addition, and Subtraction

Fostering Children's Mathematical Development, Grades PreK–3

The Landscape of Learning

FACILITATOR'S GUIDE

Antonia Cameron

Sherrin B. Hersch

Catherine Twomey Fosnot

HEINEMANN
Portsmouth, NH

Heinemann
A division of Reed Elsevier Inc.
361 Hanover Street
Portsmouth, NH 03801-3912
www.heinemann.com

Offices and agents throughout the world

This material is supported in part by the National Science Foundation under Grant No. 9911841. Any opinions, findings, and conclusions or recommendations expressed in these materials are those of the authors and do not necessarily reflect the views of the National Science Foundation.

Cataloguing-in-publication data on file at the Library of Congress.
ISBN: 0-325-00674-1

Editor: Victoria Merecki
Text and cover design: Catherine Hawkes/Cat & Mouse
Manufacturing: Jamie Carter

Printed in the United States of America on acid-free paper
07   06   05   04   T&C   1   2   3   4   5

NATIONAL FIELD TEST PARTNERS

Victoria Bill
   Learning Research and Development Center
   Institute for Learning, University of Pittsburgh
Cathy Feughlin
   The Webster Grove School District
   St. Louis, Missouri
Ginger Hanlon, Sarah Ryan, Gary Shevell
   CSD #2, New York, New York
Gretchen Johnson
   City College of New York
   School of Education
Ellen Knudson
   Bismarck, North Dakota,
   Public Schools
Charlotte Stadler
   New Rochelle, New York
   Public Schools
Sheri Willebrand
   Santa Barbara, California
   County Education Office

Linda Coutts
   Columbia, Missouri, Public Schools
Cynthia Garland-Dore
   Aspen Elementary School
   Aspen, Colorado
Bill Jacob
   University of California, Santa Barbara
Judit Kerekes
   College of Staten Island, New York
Connie Lewis
   Tucson, Arizona,
   Public Schools
Wendy Watkins Thomson
   University of Missouri, Columbia, Missouri
   Project Construct, Missouri

EVALUATION TEAM

Joseph Glick, *Director*
Mara Heppen, *Researcher*
Stephanie Domenici Cabonargi, *Researcher*

VIDEO PRODUCTION

Cathrine Kellison, Roseville Video, *Producer*
Kiyash Monsef, *Co-Producer*
Jeffrey McLaughlin, *Editor*

VIDEO CREW

John Bianchi, Tami Evioni, Richard Henning, John Javakian, Michael Kelly, Anthony McGowan, Serafin Menduina, Mark Petracca, Ben Vandenboom, Richard Westlein

Contents

Overview ix
Introduction xi

🗁 **INTERVIEWS** 1

🗁 **ROUTINES** 6

🗁 **MINILESSONS** 12

🗁 **GAMES** 21

🗁 **INVESTIGATIONS** 26

🗁 **CREATING A LANDSCAPE OF LEARNING** 39

Appendix A: Interview Transcript *(Seven Candies in a Tin)* 43
Appendix B: Games 46
Appendix C: Handy Guide to the CD-ROM Clips 49
Appendix D: Dialogue Boxes 51

Overview

Landscapes of learning is a metaphor we have chosen to characterize children's mathematical development. The metaphor of a landscape evokes a picture of a learning terrain through which pre-kindergartners, and first, second, and third graders move in meandering or direct ways as they develop number sense, addition, and subtraction. On a young child's journey there are moments of uncertainty and of potential shifts in their understanding *(crossroads)* and moments where mathematical ideas or strategies are constructed *(landmarks)*. Knowledge of these moments gives teachers the capacity to better understand, document, and stretch students' thinking. Thus, mapping out a landscape of such crossroads and landmarks can guide teachers in their planning and teaching.

Landscapes can be seen as a kind of learning trajectory—a blueprint containing guidelines for offering students learning opportunities for the development of mathematics—big ideas, models, and strategies (i.e., for number and operation). Landscapes can serve as important developmental landmarks for teachers to notice and use as they plan and as they journey with their children. They can also be used for assessment or documentation of learning. This perspective is in contrast to the viewpoint often used by curriculum developers, who perceive of curriculum as a tightly choreographed set of activities along a scope and sequence, prescribed for the teacher to follow.

As teachers design contexts for children to explore, the goal is to enable them to *mathematize*, to act on and within situations mathematically, using the landmark strategies. These progressive schematizations are the steps in the journey. The contexts are also designed to facilitate discussion around big ideas because these landmarks indicate major shifts in perspective and in cognitive restructuring. As children model and represent their strategies (e.g., on a number line) and as they develop generalized mental models of the part-whole relations for situations and operations, they construct mental maps that can eventually become powerful tools for mathematical thinking. Accordingly, assessment should document where a child is on the journey—where the child is on the landscape.

In contrast to the other CD-ROMs in the package, the *Landscape of Learning* CD-ROM contains a series of mathematical contexts embedded in short clips taken from longer clinical interviews, routines, minilessons, games, and investigations across the full grade span, PK–3. The clips have been chosen to highlight a variety of moments showing children's mathematical constructions and verbal and/or physical explanations of their mathematical understanding; to provide focused opportunities for teachers to observe, analyze, and discuss critical moments in children's development; and then to build for themselves a landscape of learning for early number sense, addition, and subtraction.

The purpose of the CD-ROM is

- to deepen viewers' ability to describe children's physical actions in relation to what they say and do, and to understand how these actions are connected to their thinking;
- to deepen viewers' ability to assess children's mathematical development and to find evidence in the CD-ROM clips for their analyses of children's mathematical activity;
- to build a landscape of the ideas, strategies, and models of early number, addition, and subtraction from what viewers see the children constructing or about to construct.

Introduction

Depending on the audience, the time frame for using the materials (a full-day workshop versus a semester's course work), and the intention behind their use, the CD-ROMs and corresponding books of the *Young Mathematicians at Work* series can be used in a variety of ways. They can be used with preservice and inservice teachers, with teacher educators, with parents, and with administrators. While we cannot predict all the possible uses of these materials and do not want to prescribe *how* facilitators will use them, we do envision *two kinds of journeys* for participants.

JOURNEY 1

In *Journey 1*, participants work through the entire CD-ROM, beginning with the pages in the first folder, "Interviews," and ending with the last folder, "Investigations." They begin by entering a virtual classroom where they experience a series of short clips of pre-kindergarten children answering questions about *how many candies;* then they can enter many other digital environments where they will see pre-kindergartners, kindergartners, first graders, second graders, and third graders all at work answering How many? (How many children, how many milks, how many blocks, how many snap cubes, how many years older, etc.) This early number sense work extends into the operations of addition and subtraction.

On the surface, *Journey 1* is sequential in nature, somewhat like reading a book from cover to cover. It is important to remember, though, that individual explorations will not be linear. *How* participants *read the book*—the thoughts and questions they raise as they move through the digital classrooms—will determine what paths they take in this journey. As a facilitator, you will set the boundaries—where the journey will begin and end. This is the power and beauty of the virtual classroom—it accommodates the needs and ideas of *all* learners simultaneously. Because learners can revisit the clips over and over, they have an opportunity to rethink their initial ideas and deepen their own understanding of children's mathematical development.

In this process, participants will also be confronting contradictions that will naturally arise from *different interpretations* of what they are seeing. As participants interact with their peers, they often have to confront their own beliefs about what they think children are doing, what they think children know. When contradictions arise in what people see—as they invariably will—revisiting the CD-ROM for supporting evidence pushes participants to distinguish between interpretation and observation.

Because they can revisit the same clips again and again, there is opportunity for participants' perceptions to deepen and change. *Reviewing* allows for *reseeing;* they can *move beyond surface interpretations and dig for deeper meaning.* This is a powerful way to develop participants' mathematical and pedagogical repertoire. As one participant wrote in a reflective journal at the end of the first in a series of workshops:

> *What's puzzling me—and what I'm going to be thinking about for some time to come—is how we can all be watching the same video clip, and yet be seeing such radically different things! If we can't agree on what we're seeing—and this is just the actions and words of two students—how can we possibly interpret what these actions and words mean?*

JOURNEY 2

In *Journey 2,* participants reenter the digital environments, but this time with a different purpose. Now they use these clips to build a *Landscape of Learning.* In *Journey 1,* participants focused on *how* to look at students, analyzed their strategies, and probed for the mathematical meaning behind these.

In order to design a Landscape of Learning, participants now must begin to synthesize their observations and analyses, look for connections between strategies, and think about the relationships of these to important mathematical ideas. As they are called upon to select moments to paste on their clipboards, to make annotations, and to place these on a landscape of learning for early number, addition, and subtraction, the pages in the CD-ROM will guide them. All of these pages are designed to help participants organize and play with their ideas. Here they can use footage and children's work that they have placed on the clipboard. They can select moments from the footage and paste them in the text as hyperlinks to illustrate their annotations. From these annotations, they can begin to build a Landscape of Learning. The creation of their *own* landscape for mathematical development is a powerful tool that helps them reflect on student strategies and think about how mathematical ideas are connected and developed over time by learners.

TECH TIP 1

For a more detailed analysis of how to build a Landscape of Learning, see the Help file in the Tools menu of the CD-ROM.

TECH TIP 2

You will find it important to not only read through the Help file on the CD-ROM, but also to practice using the technology before you begin your work with participants. Many facilitators have found it helpful to participants to print the help pages as participants' needs arose.

Journey 1

Seven Candies in a Tin

Cathy Fosnot or Maarten Dolk talk with pre-kindergartners. They are shown a closed tin that contains seven candies. On this page you can see Peter, a four-year-old, during the whole interview with Cathy. Make notes about the interview, Cathy's questions, and Peter's answers. Describe what Peter does, and what he knows about number. Why do you think Cathy asks the questions when she does?

The interviews with pre-kindergarten students in *Seven Candies in a Tin* offer participants an opportunity to think about the development of young children's counting strategies as well as provide a window into some critical big ideas in early number. The different clips of students (there are one full-length interview and eight fragments taken from other interviews) are all rooted in the question, How many candies are in the tin? This question, however, changes over the course of the interview.

In the initial context, students can count the candies in the tin to answer the question, How many . . . ? Though each child uses a counting strategy to solve the problem, there are differences in *how they do this* (e.g., taking the candies out of the tin and counting each one; counting the candies poured out on the table, but not touching them). The main thrust of this part of the clinical interview is for each student to figure out the total number of candies and then, when re-asked the same question, How many candies is that? to know that the answer *is* the quantity just counted. That the seven candies they have just counted indicate the group or set of candies and not the seventh candy, is a big idea in early number—cardinality.

Once the cardinality of the set has been established, the interviewer shifts the context slightly. It is still about candies, but now the candies are being shared with friends (e.g., if you have four friends, how many candies will you need so each friend has a candy?). Through this question, the interviewer probes a child's understanding of one-to-one correspondence, another big idea in early number. If a child knows that the number of candies needed is the same as the number of friends, the underlying big idea is one-to-one correspondence.

FACILITATION TIP 1

When we use the word *students* we are referring to the pre-K–3 children. *Participants* refers to the adult learners—e.g., preservice and inservice teachers.

1

The interview continues within this sharing context, but now candies are being removed from the tin one by one. The interviewer takes a candy out of the tin, gives it to the child, covers the lid, and asks, "Now how many candies are in the tin?" There is a *constraint* included in this new situation: the candies in the tin can no longer be counted by the students to answer the question, How many?

This is a truly problematic situation that moves the students away from physically interacting with materials to mentally acting on them. What makes this abstraction incredibly difficult for young children is that in order to solve the problem, they must think about several things simultaneously. They must consider the part removed from the tin in relationship to the whole quantity. The group of seven has now been split into two parts: the part they are holding and the other, unseen and uncountable, contained in the tin.

What does a child need to know in order to solve this problem? First, a child has to be able to conserve the quantity of the set, to know that the total amount does not change because the set is split into two groups. In whatever way the candy is shared (in this instance what is on the table and what is in the tin), the total amount of candy never changes. Seven can be seen as 1 and 6; 2 and 5; 3 and 4, and so on.

Understanding conservation allows a child to manipulate—decompose—numbers into smaller pieces. A second critical big idea a child needs to construct in order to decompose numbers into different parts is hierarchical inclusion—the idea that numbers are nested inside each other, that inside 7 is 6 and 5 and 4 and 3 and 2 and 1.

But there is yet a third big idea that can surface as students work with this problem. In order to think of the one candy on the table and figure out how many candies remain in the tin, a child has to have constructed part-whole relationships—that when one part of the whole is removed, what remains must, when put together with the missing piece, equal the total. At the heart of this action is reversibility of thinking, $1 + ? = 7$, a huge developmental shift for children on the landscape of learning for early number and one of the important models for subtraction.

There are many layers in the interview between Cathy and Peter that need to be examined by participants.[1] The context and structure of the interview has been created by Cathy to bring certain mathematical ideas to the fore (counting strategies, cardinality, one-to-one correspondence, conservation, hierarchical inclusion, and part-whole relationships). This is the surface level of the interview; the one that an interviewer *can* plan. There is, however, one key element of the interview that *cannot* be planned—the child's responses to the questions.

At the heart of the interview process is an interactive dynamic whose essence is unpredictable. Herein lies the difficulty and challenge in doing such an interview—it is not just about asking questions; it is about asking questions in relationship to a child's actions and words so that the questions can become a window into the child's mathematical development. In order to do this, the interviewer must juggle several things simultaneously: keep the goals of the interview in mind (What am I going for?); be in tune with the child, observing every detail of behavior; and recognize the mathematical ideas that underlie a child's strategies and struggles.

The subtleties of the interview that are embodied in the interactive dynamic between Cathy and Peter may initially be difficult for participants to recognize. One way to help them deal with this complexity is to have repeated viewings of the interview, but to focus each viewing on a different aspect (to see how one facilitator used this, see "Dialogue Box A: *Seven Candies in a Tin*" in Appendix D, page 51).

Perhaps the first go-around might be just to observe Peter: What are his actions? What are his words? What does Peter know mathematically? What struggles does Peter have? Can you give evidence to support what you are saying?

As participants focus on Peter, they will not be able to consider his answers without thinking about the role Cathy's questions play in the interview. Participants will also need to think about *why* Cathy asks the questions *when* she does. Some participants

---

[1]The interview transcript can be found in Appendix A, page 43.

may notice how in tune Cathy is to Peter—her responses are *in the moment* and connected to what he is doing and saying—yet they may not realize that another factor is influencing her decision making as an interviewer. She knows where she is going with her questions because the overall structure of the interview has been carefully designed. The foundation of this structure is Cathy's knowledge of mathematical development, how big ideas and strategies are connected on the landscape of learning.

The question central to the interview is How many candies? It is altered at key junctures (e.g., places in the interview where the situation shifts) to examine Peter's understanding of different mathematical ideas. In the beginning of the interview, the question, How many? examines Peter's counting strategies and understanding of cardinality. The question changes in the next segment to bring up one-to-one correspondence (one candy each for him and his three friends). In the final part of the interview, this question is used to probe Peter's construction of part-whole relationships (How many candies are in the tin now?).

Each time Peter counts the candies (whether in the tin or on the table), Cathy repeats the question, "how many is that?" At first his response to this question is to recount the candies, "1, 2 . . . 8." Once he has counted the candies, however, from that point on he answers Cathy's question with the total amount. Peter has constructed cardinality and knows that the last number he counted names the set.

When Cathy puts the candies back in the tin, she re-asks the question, "How many is that?" She offers Peter the tin in case he needs to count the candies inside. He does begin to count them, "One, two," but stops himself and says, "seven." On the surface this question appears to be the same, but it has been asked within a different context, and here, it is to determine conservation.

Prior to this, Peter has named his friends and pulled aside four candies for himself and his three buddies, demonstrating that he has one-to-one correspondence. The set of seven was split into two groups: one for him and his friends (four candies removed from the seven) and the remaining candies (this quantity was not established). Before moving on in the interview, Cathy reestablishes the total.

FACILITATION TIP 2

The interview with Peter and Cathy Fosnot will help participants understand the context of the short clips on the next interview page. *Because* the clips are so brief, when seen out of the full context it is easy for participants—especially those who are inexperienced kid watchers—to miss the *mathematics embedded in the strategies* and resort to comparing and labeling the students (e.g., *Sydney is bright; Shatisha is slow*). If this occurs, it is important to remind participants that these shorter clips are only snapshots of children, pieces of a larger picture taken out of context, and as such are only glimpses into their development; and that such labels and global evaluations are not helpful in describing learning and may be detrimental. One child may walk sooner than another, who may talk first. Development in one domain, such as mathematics, should not be confused with intelligence. While we *can* analyze the children's strategies in terms of mathematical development, these brief moments *cannot* be used to make sweeping generalizations about their overall understanding and/or ability.

The full-length interview with Peter is multifaceted and rich in detail. There are many elements to consider simultaneously that may initially prove overwhelming to participants but are important nonetheless. As in all their work on the CD-ROM, participants will be *kid watching,* thinking about a child's actions and words and the connection of these to mathematical big ideas. But now there is another, important facet to consider: the role of the interviewer and how this dynamic probes student thinking and brings ideas and strategies to the surface for examination.

In the shorter clips the role of the interviewer cannot clearly be discerned. So while participants can focus on the students' strategies in the shorter clips, *how and why* these strategies occur cannot be understood because the too-brief interactive dynamic between the interviewer and the child cannot be fully examined.

In the complete interview, the structure of the conversation is controlled by Cathy Fosnot's questions. Her questions are rooted in the mathematical ideas she is trying to investigate. Thus, Peter's actions and words do not occur in a vacuum, but are connected to the questions he is asked. It is equally important, however, for participants to recognize that while Cathy is controlling the discussion, her questions are not arbitrary, but are intimately connected to Peter's responses and behaviors. They are her way of probing Peter's thinking to understand his mathematical development.

The important role Cathy plays as an interviewer, the types of questions she asks, and the careful, skillful way she uses them to understand Peter's thinking may not immediately be apparent to participants. One way to help them deal with the complexity of the dialogue dance is to have repeated viewings, and to focus their attention on different aspects of the interview. Eventually, what seems like separate threads (e.g., the questions and role of the interviewer, the student's strategies—both words and actions), can be woven together to form a more complete picture.

The dynamics of the interview, the interaction between Peter and Cathy, the shifting of questions based on his actions and words, how she probes his mathematical thinking—all of these are important elements, critical to understanding the interview. Peter's actions are connected to a carefully structured interview, in which the ideas and strategies examined cannot be separated from the questions asked. These details, however, may be too subtle for participants to notice.

Here, Peter's recognition that the total has not changed is a clue that he has constructed conservation as well as cardinality.

In the next part of the interview, the tin is closed. Thus, while the context is the same—sharing candies with his three friends (all the candies have been put back in the tin and are removed one at a time)—there is now a constraint that restricts him from physically counting the candies. The only candies he holds (and can count or subitize) are the ones on the table. The ones in the tin are hidden and uncountable.

How difficult this is for a young child is reflected in Peter's face as he ponders the question, How many are in the tin now? That he can keep track of what is left in the tin as candies are removed is rooted in an understanding of three big ideas in early number: conservation of number (the total does not change as the set is split into two groups); hierarchical inclusion (numbers nest inside each other, thus a number can be split into different parts); and part-whole relationships (figuring out what is left in the tin by thinking simultaneously about the candy on the table in relationship to the total number of candies and the missing piece being a quantity that, when put together with the candy on the table, will equal seven).

FACILITATION TIP 3

↗ Give the participants the transcript (Appendix A: "Interview Transcript: *Seven Candies in a Tin*," page 43) and ask them to focus on a number of things simultaneously: the interaction between Peter and Cathy, the kinds of questions she asked, the structure of the interview, and what information the transcript can give them about Peter. Recognize that this will be a difficult task for participants, but reading a transcript will help them isolate the structure of the interview and focus on other details. Watching the interview adds many distractions—the physical actions, facial expressions, the interactive dynamic coming to life. Sample dialogue for this activity is provided in Appendix D, page 51.

Even though other subtleties in this interview may initially elude participants, these are important to bring up for discussion. For example, at no point in the interview does Cathy ask Peter to count. Even when he has miscounted the candies in the tin twice, she doesn't interfere with his actions (show him how to count) or say, "No, that's wrong." She spills the candies out on the table and says, "You want to check again?" This type of interaction occurs later, when Cathy asks Peter how many friends he has (after he has named them, Deron, Jared, and Herb). When he responds, "four," she does not correct him, but paraphrases what he says, "You think it's four," and invites him to recheck his answer when she lists the names. Peter begins to count the names as Cathy recites them, and he self-corrects the number of friends to three.

Because many of the interview threads delineated above will not be immediately recognized by participants, the focus questions listed below can be helpful during discussions of the interview:

- What role does questioning play in supporting and probing a student's strategies?

- Why does Cathy keep asking the same question, "How many . . . ?" How does this question change over the course of the interview?

- What is the structure of the interview? How does this structure bring students' ideas to the surface?

- What are Peter's strategies to solve the question, How many candies? (Give specific examples from his actions and/or words.) Do his strategies change? If so, how?

- What role does context play in this interview? How does it support development?

- What constraints have been built into the interview? How do they stretch student thinking?

Seven Candies: Shatisha, Sydney, and Deron

◉ *On this page you will see shorter clips of the same interview with three more preschoolers from the same class: Shatisha, Sydney, and Deron. Describe each child's actions and words. What mathematical ideas and strategies are they using?*

The clips on this page offer different views of children's struggles and successes with the various guises of the How many question. These clips can be compared with Peter's interview. Some key questions to use as participants watch and analyze them are:

- What actions do students use to count the candies? How are they similar? How are they different?
- Why might counting candies in the tin be difficult for students?
- What affects students' counting? Why might they be getting different answers for the same amount?
- What organizing strategies do the students use to help them keep track as they count?
- What are children's struggles? How are their struggles similar or different?
- How are children's struggles a reflection of the mathematical ideas they are constructing?

While each student counts the candies to find out how many, *how* they count is different. Shatisha (Clip 48)[2] takes the candies out of the tin, carefully counting each one slowly and methodically. Her voice is in synchrony with her action as she removes the candy from the tin. Compare this with Peter (Clip 46), who pushes the candies away from himself as he counts, or with Deron (Clip 99), who keeps the candies bunched in a pile and tags each candy without separating what he has counted from the group. All three students tag the candies as they count; Sydney (Clips 50 and 51), on the other hand, never touches the candies at all (even when they are in the tin). When the candies are spread out on the table, she accurately counts them without physically touching them.

After they have counted the candies, all of the children answer the repeated question, How many? with the name of the set. Yet in Clip 48, Shatisha, when re-asked this question (the candies are encased in the tin and cannot be touched) counts by rote beyond seven, which hints that perhaps, for her, the How many question is more about rote counting than an understanding of quantity. Cardinality is still on the horizon for Shatisha as evidenced in Clip 49, when she holds a candy in her hand and recounts the ones left in the tin ("1, 2, 3 . . . 13"). Her lack of organization (a big idea in early number)—not knowing where she starts and ends—makes her keep counting those she has already counted. The absence of puzzlement—in these three short clips she gives three different answers, 7, 16, and 13, two of them larger than the original set she counted—hints that Shatisha is still constructing cardinality; she does not yet recognize that once the set is counted the number she ends on is the amount of the set (cardinality) and that no matter how the amount is arranged, it stays the same (conservation).

Sydney (Clip 98), like Peter, has constructed part-whole relationships. She keeps track of the total amount as she figures out the quantity left in the tin in relationship to the candy she holds in her hand. Deron (Clip 100) is still constructing this idea; he establishes the parts of the set (two in his hand and five in the tin), but when asked, "How many is that altogether?" does not know that the parts will equal the total, seven.

Backburner

◎ *This is the last page of the folder "Interviews." However, you may have other questions on this topic that you would like to investigate. Go to the TOOLS menu above and add them to your backburner notes.*

The *Backburner* page is a tool for *both* participants and facilitators. As participants work with the materials, they may raise many questions that may not be easily or immediately answered. The *Backburner* page offers them a place to keep their questions for another time. These may be answered or evolve as they work more deeply with the CD-ROM.

---

[2]A handy guide to the video clips and their location on the CD-ROM (e.g., Clip 48, Interviews, Seven Candies: Shatisha, Sydney and Deron) is in Appendix C.

The digital learning environment can be the context for further investigations, which can be rooted in the learner's own questions. A facilitator can use participants' questions to form study groups; participants with similar questions (e.g., How do different students in Jodi's class record the quantity they have counted? How does notation develop? Are some students more vocal than others? What are the power relationships in pairs? Is one child more dominant? etc.) can research them. (Some additional reading materials are provided under INFO in the menu bar.)

For a facilitator, participants' questions can be a window to their thinking, offering invaluable insights into beliefs. Yet in a discussion questions might very well derail the focus. A beautiful way to validate the importance of individual ponderings but not alter the flow of discourse is to encourage the use of the *Backburner* page (e.g., What a wonderful question! We won't be able to think about it right now, but if you put it on the backburner, perhaps we can think about it at another time.). In looking at questions recorded on the *Backburner* page, a facilitator can also see the evolution of a participant's thinking. It is helpful to note: Do their questions change as they work with the materials? If so, how?

ROUTINES

Attendance Chart

⊚ *With an attendance chart (built like a* rekenrek*) the students in Kathy Sillman's first-grade class determine how many children are present. What strategies might the children use?*

On this page is a picture of Kathy sitting in front of an attendance chart structured to bring ideas about ten up for discussion. Because teachers must submit a daily count of how many children are present and absent, the routine of taking attendance lends itself exceptionally well to being used mathematically to answer the question, How many? The mathematical ideas that have shaped Kathy's chart are the ten structure of our number system and the smaller groups of five and five within ten.

On the LCD, show the pictures of Kathy's chart:

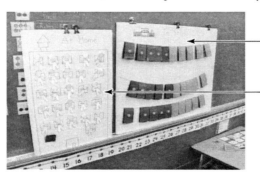

Attendance Routine:

When the children come in each morning, they put their figures on the *Attendance* chart.

When they leave at the end of the day, they put their figures on the *At Home* chart.

and in front of her attendance chart:

How many children are in class today?

Have participants take some time to examine the chart—based on a *rekenrek*[3]—and ask them to describe how they would answer the question How many children are here today? They might use:

- the number of children shapes on each row;
- the number of rows;
- the colors on each row;
- the colors on each side;
- or a combination of ways.

Use what participants say in a conversation to tease out their anticipation of the first-grade students' possible strategies to find out how many children are present. What are these potential strategies?

- students can count by ones to twenty-six,
- they can skip count by fives (5, 10, 15, 20, 25) and add one more,
- they can skip count by tens to twenty, then count on six more; or skip count by tens to twenty, then add on five more and then one more, or
- some children might reason that if all the rows were filled, there would be thirty and count backward from thirty to the red one (29, 28, 27, 26 . . .)

You can draw upon the strategies participants say children might use to engage participants in a discussion of the difficulties these strategies might present—what difficulties might arise when children switch from one counting strategy to another, such as going from skip counting by fives and adding one more.

Working with the Attendance Chart

◎ *In the following clips you see two children from Kathy's first-grade class investigating the number of children represented on the attendance chart. What mathematical ideas and strategies are they using? What mathematical struggles do they have?*

In the two clips on this page participants have a chance to see how the children use the attendance chart. You may wish to focus their small-group viewing on how the structure of the attendance chart supports each boy's organization and counting strategy. What can they say about the boys' ideas and struggles? Having them imitate for each other the physical actions of each of the boys may be helpful in moving participants toward

---

[3]For using the *rekenrek* with routines, we refer you to *Young Mathematicians at Work: Constructing Number Sense, Addition, and Subtraction*, pp. 109–12.

FACILITATION TIP 4

The "Routines" folder and the activities listed below all contain contexts that are enhanced by the structure of the *rekenrek*, the Dutch name for arithmetic rack. You will see, for example, how it is used as an attendance chart, as a bunk bed, and as a double-decker bus to develop young children's emergent ideas and strategies of early number in the following activities:

Attendance (first grade)

Attendance (kindergarten)

Bunk-Bed Stories (kindergarten)

Double-Decker Buses (first grade)

Milks (pre-kindergarten)

It will be important, then, for participants to gain working knowledge of the *rekenrek*. You can have them read about (We refer you to *Young Mathematicians at Work, Number Sense, Addition, and Subtraction,* pp. 105–09.), and explore with them the ten structure of its two rows of five red, five white beads—working with an actual *rekenrek* in part of a session with participants, and studying and discussing Brigida Littles' modeling of it in the *Double-Decker Bus* page on the LCD.

The picture below shows a class-size *rekenrek,* from the activity, *Double-Decker Buses.* Notice that the teacher has moved the beads to the left side of the *rekenrek,* red beads first, then white. This is so children will "read" them in the left-to-right orientation already familiar to them in reading and writing. Sample dialogue for this is provided in Appendix D, page 53.

describing children in positive ways rather than in deficit ways (e.g., "The boy has no organization.").

Kathy's questioning not only supports the children's learning, but children's answers also give her clues about their thinking. For example, when she asks in Clip 17, "How did you see that this was six without having to count?" the boy says, "I knew that five [touches the group] and one [touches it] is six." He uses the five as a unit and adds one more to it.

Attendance in Kindergarten

◉ *In Shanna Schwartz's kindergarten class the students use an attendance chart also. We see Alexa figuring out how many lizards have been placed on the green part of the attendance chart.*

In the picture of Alexa at the board (to be viewed in Clip 91), we glimpse a bit of the green side of Shanna Schwartz's kindergarten attendance chart. Like Kathy, she has arranged her chart in three rows of ten, each row consisting of five yellow and five green spaces. (Notice the little circles of Velcro where the children can attach their iguanas.)

Before participants watch Clip 91, you might ask them to watch and take notes with these foci in mind: (1) the arrangement of the iguanas on the green side, and (2) how Alexa organizes her counting (this suggestion might ensure that participants focus on Alexa's actions and words—what she is doing—rather than on what she is *not doing*).

Arrangement of the Iguanas, Green Side. The black dots below represent the iguanas on the right (green) side of the chart. What are some possible ways they can be counted?

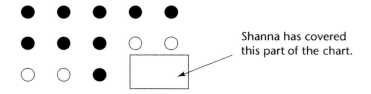

Shanna has covered this part of the chart.

Participants' responses might be that children will

- count by ones, moving left to right from row to row, top to bottom;
- see the five on the top row and count on the iguanas on the next row, 6, 7, 8, then count the iguana on the bottom row, 9;

- move the bottom iguana to the space next to the third iguana in the second row, so that the configuration is 5, top row, and 4, middle row. Students can then subitize the 5 in the top row and count on 6, 7, 8, 9, or

- reason that if the first and second row were filled there would be ten iguanas, but one is not there, so ten less one are 9 iguanas.

When the clip begins, Alexa has answered, from where all the children are seated, that she thinks there are six iguanas on the right. Shanna invites Alexa to come up to the chart and asks, "Six where, on the bottom, or the green iguanas? Can you show us what you mean?" (to clarify what "on the right" means).

How does Alexa organize her count? The numbered arrangement below shows her counting path. She starts at the bottom:

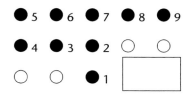

"Are you sure?" (Shanna asks this question because Alexa stopped after "4" and said, "actually . . . ?)

Shanna asks a series of questions that are connected to Alexa's actions:

Do you want to change your answer? (letting Alexa know that she *can* change)

Do you want to show us again? (inviting Alexa to try again)

Alexa counts a second time, using the existing arrangement and the same counting path, but now she includes all the iguanas:

Although it is hard to see her tag and hear her say "6, 7," Alexa ends at "8, 9" and tells Shanna and the class that there are nine.

> *Shanna:* How many? *(asking to tease out cardinality)*
>
> *Alexa:* Nine.

Attendance Stick

◉ *Together the students in Shanna's class find that there are twenty-four children in the class today. Now they figure how to make their attendance stick represent the number of children present.*

The attendance stick referred to above is part of classroom routines in the TERC *Investigations* curriculum.[4] Just as there are twenty-eight iguana spaces for the twenty-eight children in the class on the attendance chart, Shanna's attendance stick has a length of twenty-eight connected snap cubes of one color.

---

[4] TERC *Investigations in Number, Data, and Space, Mathematical Thinking in Kindergarten, About Classroom Routines.*

Shanna has two parts to her attendance routine: the attendance chart and the attendance stick. Some questions to ask are:

- How are the two connected?
- How will using them both support development?

Shanna has incorporated a big idea in early number of one-to-one correspondence by including the attendance stick in her routine. Having taken attendance, the children know that twenty-four children are present. The ways in which children figure out how to make the stick match the chart data indicate whether they have constructed this big idea. There is a subtle difference between one-to-one matching and one-to-one correspondence. When Shanna asks, "Can you make the stick match [the chart]?" she is not suggesting a matching strategy (e.g., one iguana/one cube, two iguanas/two cubes, and then counting to see how many cubes you have). A child who has constructed one-to-one correspondence knows without counting, without matching, that if there are twenty-four iguanas, the stick should also show twenty-four cubes.

Before they watch the clip, ask participants to think about potential strategies children might use to make the attendance stick match the chart: for example, a child might count the cubes by ones to 24 and break off the rest of the cubes.

In Clip 92, the boy's strategy is to look at how many iguanas are *not* on the chart. He says, "Those are the four iguanas that are absent." His one-to-one correspondence is with the absentees. He makes the stick match the chart by removing *four cubes*. "Take off from the stick." (Note: Participants often think that this strategy is very advanced because they view what he is doing as subtraction. But actually all he is doing is noting four and removing them. Subitizing is sufficient to be able to do this. So the juxtaposition of these two clips can be used to discuss the thinking behind the strategies—to push participants to reflect deeply. They often compare him to Alexa, whom they see as struggling.)

When the chart is filled, there are twenty-eight children, and the boy has seen the four empty spaces (one yellow and three green). The attendance stick contains twenty-eight cubes, so he pulls four cubes off the stick. He has not counted twenty-four cubes, but knows that four iguanas not here are four cubes to be removed ("not here") and then the stick will "match" the chart.

Shanna asks: "How many are you going to take off? Why are you going to take off four?" And she paraphrases the boy's statement about the absent iguanas: "So if four iguanas are not there, you knew that four kids are absent?" (The boy nods.)

Milks in Pre-kindergarten

◎ *In Diane Jackson's pre-kindergarten class, the students investigate how many milks are needed for all the children. The attendance rack shows the number of children present. Several students have taken attendance. There are sixteen children present. Diane asks Keshawn, How many milks are needed for sixteen children? Observe Keshawn, Arkell, and Herb. What are your noticings?*

The three- and four-year-old children in Diane Jackson's class are familiar with an ongoing milk routine that relates to their attendance chart. Diane's chart is modeled after the *rekenrek* in that it also has two rows, each with five red and five white pockets. Her purpose is to use this five structure to support the development of strategies other than counting by ones. Every day the children put "themselves" (little boy/girl dolls) into these pockets as part of the morning routine.

Before watching Clips 211 and 212, you might show participants Diane's attendance chart and ask what strategies they conjecture pre-kindergartners might use to figure out *how many* boys, girls, and children are present. Their recent experience with the children in *Seven Candies in a Tin* should be helpful to them as they answer your question. They might anticipate that children will:

- use a range of individual counting organizations;
- tag each figure with voices in/not in synchrony;
- use the number sequence in a range of fluency counting to sixteen; or
- double tag some objects, or skip some;
- know when they reach eleven that there are eleven boys;
- know when they reach sixteen that there are sixteen children; or
- count from one again if they lose count, etc.

Because boy and girl figures are placed randomly, Herb (Clip 211) must be careful to count just the boys (there are eleven). Diane asks, "How many?" Herb says, "Eleven."

Once the attendance count of sixteen children is determined by Arkell (Clip 212), Diane asks (Clip 55), "Keshawn, how many milks will we need for sixteen children?"

Backburner

◉ *This is the last page in the folder, "Routines." However, you may have other questions on this topic that you would like to investigate. Go to the TOOLS menu above and add them to your backburner notes.*

See *Backburner* notes, page 5.

ACTIVITY 1   Comparing Attendance Charts

✂ Now that participants have studied the attendance routines in Diane's pre-K, Shanna's kindergarten, and Kathy's first grade, you may wish to set aside some class time for them to work in their small groups to compare and contrast the three *rekenrek* charts the teachers have created. Showing the three charts side by side may help participants to analyze them for similarities and differences.

Pre-K Attendance Chart. Two rows of five red, five white pockets, affixed to the chart.

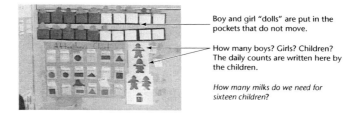

Boy and girl "dolls" are put in the pockets that do not move.

How many boys? Girls? Children? The daily counts are written here by the children.

How many milks do we need for sixteen children?

Kindergarten Attendance Chart. Three rows of five yellow, five green rectangles, affixed to the chart. (Shanna covered the last two boxes because the children asked her to.)

Children place their iguanas on the Velcro dots. *How many children are here today?*

Can we make the attendance stick match the attendance chart?

First-grade Attendance Chart. Three rows of five blue, five red rectangles that are strung so that they can be moved.

Children move their figures from the *At Home* chart to the *Attendance* Chart each morning

How many children are here today?

Some focusing questions for participants can be:

- What potential mathematical ideas do each of the charts support?
- What are the potential strategies that children can use to find out how many are here today?
- Discuss how Diane's recording routine, Shanna's attendance stick, and Kathy's moveable chart support and stretch children's development.

Sample dialogue for this activity is provided in Appendix D, page 53.

MINILESSONS

Playing Tag

◉ *Kathy tells her first-grade students how she observed them from the roof of the school building playing tag. From above she could see only the tops of their heads. Looking at several "snapshots" the students work out how many children are playing tag. Describe the mathematical strategies you see the children constructing.*

Young children are able to subitize *how many* there are in a small group (e.g., seeing 2, 3, 4 without having to count). In games, when they begin to use dice or play dominoes, children know *how many* without counting these familiar patterns. Yet, even so, the tried-and-true habit of counting by ones remains hard for many young children to relinquish.

FACILITATION TIP 5

The value of quick images may not be immediately apparent to many participants, who may think that figuring out how many dots is a very simple task for the first graders, or just a counting activity. One way for participants to understand how rich and important an activity it is, is for them to do some quick images as a group before they go off to watch the clips. It is well worth taking the time to prepare dot arrangements on transparencies that you can place on an overhead projector, show quickly, and ask, How many? How did you know that? Did anyone see it another way? It is also important to represent what people say, and ask, for example: Is this what you mean? If you are to represent the participant's strategy accurately, the participant needs to be precise in describing it. Here is an example of one such arrangement and some samples of representations.

Quick-image arrangement

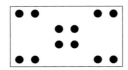

Some representations:

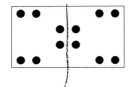 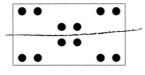 

That there can be multiple perspectives of an arrangement of dots is at the crux of quick images. Participants can begin to appreciate the number of other ways the dot arrangements can be mentally manipulated as they tell each other how they saw *how many* dots, e.g., by visualizing the snapshot in its entirety; remembering the groupings; holding the images in one's head in a particular way so that they can be mentally manipulated; using a strategy that makes sense to them. It becomes clear that the goal of the quick images, for participants as well as for children, is not merely to get the answer.

To encourage her first graders to move away from counting by ones, Kathy has created a *Playing Tag* scenario to show the class a variety of snapshot combinations of them playing tag in the school yard that she will project very quickly—too quickly to be counted by ones. The constraint of showing the dots as quick images[5], which can be subitized by the students, encourages individual student strategies and supports development at the same time.

In Clip 18, Kathy shows this snapshot and asks, "What happened?"

Willie: It's 7.

Kathy: How do you know that?

W: Because I see 4 there and 3 there.

Kathy represents what he says.

K: How does that help you?

Willie: Because I know that 3 plus 3 are 6 plus 1 more is 7.

In the dot arrangement above Willie uses a doubles plus strategy. He decomposes the 4 dots into 3 and 1; he then puts that 3 together with the other 3 (a double)

[5]For additional reading about quick images, we refer you to Chapter 6 in *Young Mathematicians at Work: Constructing Number Sense, Addition, and Subtraction.*

for 6, and says, "and 1 more is 7." What mathematical ideas has Willie constructed? The dot configuration, after all, is not 3 and 3 and 1. It is 3 and 4. In order to decompose the 4 and use the 3 + 3 as a doubling strategy, Willie is using a big idea of early number, hierarchical inclusion—that nested inside a big number are the smaller numbers that come before it in the counting sequence—as his strategy. He also understands another big idea in early number—conservation—no matter how you arrange the dots, the total amount stays the same.

In Clip 20, the 3-4 snapshot is now a 3-4-3:

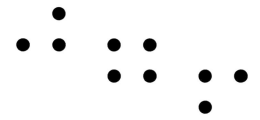

Willie draws on his understanding of the aforementioned big ideas when he says, "I know that 6 and 4 is 10, because if you added 1 more from the 6 to the 5 it would be 5 and 5." Willie decomposes the 6 into 5 and 1 and then "moves" 1 from the 6 and "gives it" to the 4, making the double 5 and 5. For participants, his mental switching can be represented (see below) to show how Willie is using a big idea of compensation as a strategy: You can remove a number from an addend and give it to the other addend without changing the total amount.

FACILITATION TIP 6

The next snapshot of the children playing tag is not shown first in Clip 21 as has been the case with the previous clips. You might take this opportunity, then, to have participants listen to the dialogue between the student and Kathy, and then push the PAUSE button on the LCD projector. Based on the clues given in the brief exchange between Kathy and the student, ask participants to confer in their groups and then draw the snapshot that they think Kathy shows the class. Each table can display and talk about their transformation of the 3-4-3 snapshot to their snapshot. Afterward, you can resume play of the clip so that they can see Kathy's.

Another student gives his explanation, "3 and 3, I know makes 6 and 4 more makes 10." Kathy circles the dots the boy has mentioned (3 and 3), as she says, "OK. So is this the 3 and 3 you saw?"

He uses the double 3 and 3 outer dots first to make 6 and adds the 4 dots in the center in last. The big idea underpinning his strategy is the associative property in

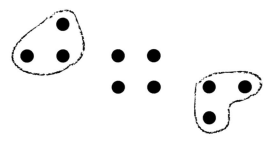

addition: you can add numbers out of the sequence they are written in without changing the sum.

Here is a snapshot in Clip 21 that shows Kathy's transformation from the 3-4-3 snapshot to a 6-4 snapshot to make the "new" shape of 6.

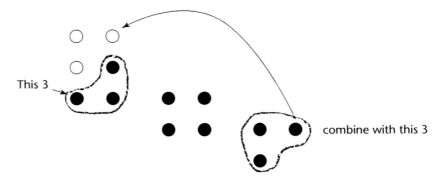

This 3

combine with this 3

Kathy represents what the student says:

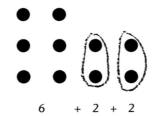

6   + 2 + 2

Bunk Bed Stories in Kindergarten

◎ *Shanna tells a story about her younger sister's birthday party. Her sister invited seven children. Each time Shanna reenters the room, the eight children are seated differently on the bunk bed. The question she repeats is: "How many children? Did I lose one?" What strategies do the children use to determine if there are still eight children?*

Shanna Schwartz is using the *rekenrek* to model a bunk bed scenario to explore with her kindergarten class the various ways that eight children can move from the top bunk to the bottom bunk (or vice versa), while the total number of children remains constant. Underpinning this minilesson string[6], exploring different combinations of eight, are big ideas in early number that are related to each other:

cardinality (the last number counted is the set);

conservation (however a quantity is arranged, the number stays the same);

part-whole relationships (as parts of a whole are rearranged, the whole doesn't change); and

compensation (if one is removed from one part and given to the other part, the total number stays the same).

As told via the bunk bed story in these very short clips, Shanna's string of combinations of eight is:

4 + 4

3 + 5

2 + 6

6 + 2

7 + 1

If you decide to write this string of related problems out for participants to examine, before they look at the clip, ask: Why might Shanna have chosen these prob-

---

[6]Refer participants to *Young Mathematicians at Work: Constructing Number Sense, Addition, and Subtraction*, pp. 127–133, on strings. Strings are a series of related computation problems governed by an overarching focus. Shanna's string is based on compensation and part-whole relationships.

lems, and in this order? How are the problems related? What might children learn from this string?

In the picture below from Clip 3, there are three "children" on the top bunk and five on the bottom bunk.

$$3 + 5 = 8$$

This kindergartner has counted three times: 1, 2, 3, 4, 5 (bottom), 1, 2, 3 (top); then 1, 2, 3 . . . 8. (Note: The *rekenrek* is usually read from the top, then the bottom, making what is seen here 3 + 5.)

The previous arrangement had been 4 + 4. Shanna has pushed one bead on the top row to the left behind the curtain and has brought one out from the bottom, moving it to the right. She makes her movements broad and visible to everyone so they can observe how the kids at the party keep moving from one part of the bed to the other (later she will invite children up to the bead frame to move the bead "children" and change the combination themselves). The children observe the transformation from 4 on the top and 4 on the bottom, to 3 on the top and 5 on the bottom. They may also notice that when 1 moves *off* the top, 1 moves *on* the bottom (or vice versa).

In Clip 4, to focus in on the movement of the bead "children," Shanna asks, "So how many kids moved from the top to the bottom?" Asisha answers, "You only moved one. You put one back [indicating the top] and you took one from here [indicating the bottom]." Shanna paraphrases and models on the *rekenrek* what Asisha, who did not physically manipulate the beads, has just explained.

The context of the bunk bed story is very real for the kindergartners (notice that Shanna stays within the context). At one moment (Clip 5) when there is a change in the *rekenrek* bunk bed, Shanna asks, "What happened, Callum?" He explains, "He went down the ladder." He uses the context to explain compensation.

The bunk bed story holds the notion for them that the number of children stays the same despite all the movement up and down, down and up, and the *rekenrek* structure allows for this fluidity of movement.

In Clip 6, Shanna asks, "Is there another way?" Here she is pushing the children to examine deeply the part-whole relations and to challenge them to consider: How many ways are there? Have we done them all? Will they develop a systematic way to prove what all the possible combinations are?

Elon goes to the *rekenrek* and moves two beads that are on the bottom to the left behind the curtain and moves one over from the top and then one over from the bottom (how interesting that he moves *two*, but then *splits them* behind the curtain and gives *one to each* bunk bed).

Shanna asks "How many now, Kyana? Before there were six on top and two on the bottom." Kyana answers, "Seven on top, one on the bottom."

⊚ *Brigida Littles, a first-grade teacher, has brought in a toy double-decker bus. She uses this context to do a minilesson with the* rekenrek.

Having worked through the attendance and milks contexts in the "Routines" folder, and the bunk bed context in the "Minilessons" folder, participants should be familiar with the structure of the *rekenrek*. They viewed kindergartners using this arithmetic rack to find out How many? and analyzed their counting strategies—*counting three times, counting by ones;* they observed kindergartners noticing that even if one child moved to the top bunk from the bottom, changing the arrangement, there were still eight children.

In this minilesson, participants will have the opportunity to note how the *rekenrek*'s structure, used as a model for a double-decker bus, has the potential to support the development of more efficient counting strategies. Here viewers can observe the range of development among first graders as they answer How many? within a bus context. The children in Brigida Littles' class are familiar with the double-decker tourist buses that drive around the city, and they know that, unlike regular city buses, passengers can sit either on top or on the bottom. As Neffertiti says, "It's like a double bus; there are seats on top and seats on the bottom" (Clip 93).

Brigida, to set the stage for the top and bottom rows of the *rekenrek*, says, "Whenever I have seen it I wonder how the bus driver knows how many people are on the top and on the bottom." The children's responses indicate that they have some fomenting ideas about this.

FACILITATION TIP 7

➚ In Clip 8, Brigida starts with a commonly known double, 5 + 5. Notice that she moves the five red beads *in one motion*, as a *group of five* (not 1, 2, 3, 4, 5), and says, "5 and 5." In fact, in Clips 9 and 10, she consistently moves beads in groups—twos, threes, fours, etc. By doing so she is encouraging the students to use groups—the fives, tens, twos, etc., that they can subitize clearly on the *rekenrek*.

We suggest that you have participants work in their small groups, in a first viewing of these eight short clips, to watch how Brigida uses the *rekenrek* and moves the beads. Ask each of them to jot down what they notice and to exchange their noticings with their group. The beauty of the clips is that they can be viewed again to settle any disagreements that arise, and participants' kid watching gets sharper as a result.

In the whole-group share, participants may have noticed that:

- all ten beads on each row (twenty beads) are at the right side from the children's point of view, before Brigida begins;
- Brigida moves beads *in groups* to the other side, and tells how many she moves (e.g., five and five); (if there are earmarks of a potentially lengthy discussion about the pros and cons of Brigida's telling, suggest that this can be put on their backburner pages for later discussion);
- students "read" the beads in a left to right orientation;
- the beads not used are also visible;
- you can see doubles—double reds or double whites—very clearly without counting by ones;
- you can know *how many* by looking at the beads that are not used, especially when the "bus" is getting full.

Arrangements on a Double-Decker Bus

⊚ *Together they explore several different settings. Each time the question is: "How many people are on the bus?" What strategies do the first-grade children use? Describe the strategy in each clip. What strategies are useful in each of the arrangements?*

Brigida is using the *rekenrek* to capitalize on the fact that its five structure can be subitized by the children—the groups of five reds (top/bottom) or five reds/five whites in a row. At the same time her focus is on doubles (Note: on the *rekenrek*, in doubles greater than five and five, there are two sets of doubles, e.g., 7 + 7 can also be viewed as 5 + 5 and 2 + 2).

Using a large *rekenrek* with a small group of first graders, Brigida shows them bead arrangements (see below) and frames her questions in relation to what the children say. Unlike Shanna, who covered one side and displayed the other side of the *rekenrek*, Brigida uses the *rekenrek* in its entirety.

Ask participants, as they watch the clips, to focus on what the children say and what questions Brigida asks. Can

	The teacher's questions:	*Children's answers:*
	How many on the bus?	*Khalil:* I know that 5 + 5 is 10.
	What if there were 6 on top?	*Neffertiti:* 11. It's like 10 + 1. (Neffertiti is using the double—(5 + 5) +1—as her strategy.)
	How did you know it was 16?	*Ralovel:* 16. There's 12, 13, 14, 15 . . . oh, it's 18.

When Ralovel (Clip 9) explains why it is 16, he reconstructs a doubles/double + 1 sequence of the people who got on the bus. First he says "6 + 6 [12] plus 1 more [13] plus 1 more [14] plus 1 more, uh . . ." He sees that there will be more than the 16 beads he said. The structure of the *rekenrek* gives him that feedback—Brigida doesn't need to—and he has the opportunity to reconsider and change his answer. (Notice that as he explains his thinking, he says, "6 and 1 (13)." He means, but is not saying, "6 and 6 *and* 1.") He does the same thing as he explains why it is 18. He says "because 5 and 5 and 4 and 4 is 8."

In the short Clips 10, 11, and 12, focus on children's explanations of how many are on the bus, as depicted below, and ask participants to analyze what big ideas or strategies they think the children have constructed. In Clips 10, 11, and 12:

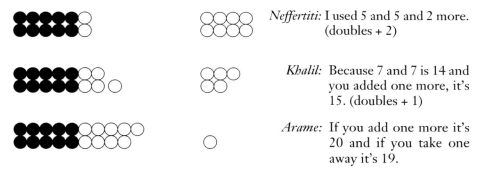

Neffertiti: I used 5 and 5 and 2 more. (doubles + 2)

Khalil: Because 7 and 7 is 14 and you added one more, it's 15. (doubles + 1)

Arame: If you add one more it's 20 and if you take one away it's 19.

Arame is looking at the one remaining bead at the right to explain how she knows it is 19. When all the beads are used, there are 20; one less is 19 *(take one away)* and if you had 19, one more would be 20 *(add one more)*. There are two big ideas here: *part-whole* (20 can be separated into 19 + 1) and *hierarchical inclusion* (19 is inside 20).

In Clips 13, 14, and 15, Brigida is modeling doubles as a strategy for children to use when they have to figure out one more (or one less) than the double (6 + 5 is 5 + 5 + 1 or is 6 + 6 – 1). Brigida is also using compensation as an idea and as a potential strategy, especially when the children can watch her as she rearranges the beads. They see that although she removes two beads from the bottom row, she puts two on the top row. They see that nothing has been removed and tell her it (the How many?) will be the same as the one before.

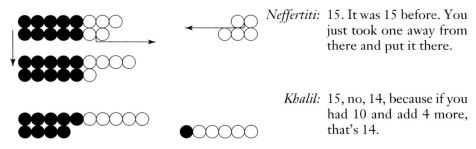

Neffertiti: 15. It was 15 before. You just took one away from there and put it there.

Khalil: 15, no, 14, because if you had 10 and add 4 more, that's 14.

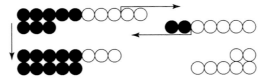

Ralovel: 13. You took 2 more away and you put 2 in. That's 10 right there, and I counted 3 more.

The students are using a big idea of compensation in the above bead actions.

43 + 20

◉ *Hildy Martin, a second-grade teacher, is doing some mental mathematics addition problems. Describe each student's strategy.*

Hildy is working with an addition problem—43 + 20—as part of a minilesson. She uses the *open number line* as a model to represent the students' *computation strategies.* (Hildy and the class constructed the number line in the course of a measurement investigation.)

Have participants do the problem before they watch the students. What strategies might they use to solve 43 + 20? They may:

- split the 43 and add 40 + 20 = 60, then add 3 (60 + 3 = 63);
- start with 43 and add 20 all at once; or
- start with 43 and split the 20 (10 + 10)—43 + 10 = 53, 53 + 10 = 63, etc.

Because the open number line may be new to participants, model its use by representing what they say, and model questioning by the way you ask them for "directions," for example, "Where did you get 40?" and by the way you ask, "Did anyone do it another way?"

Send participants off in their small groups to analyze Clip 74, Melissa's strategy, and Clip 75 to analyze Janet's and to watch how Hildy uses the open number line to represent each girl's strategy. The two strategies are:

Melissa's Strategy

- starts with 20 (changes the problem into 20 + 43; the underlying big idea is the commutative property of addition)
- splits 43 into 40 + 3
- adds 20 + 40 + 3

Hildy's representation on the open number line:

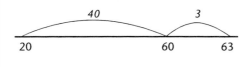

Janet's Strategy

- starts with 43
- splits 20 into 10 + 10
- adds 43 + 10 + 10 (taking jumps of 10)

Hildy's representation on the open number line:

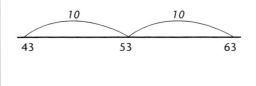

---

192 – 40

Clips 76 and 77 are snapshots of third-grade students solving a variety of subtraction problems as part of a mental math minilesson (strings).[7] The two clips, though brief, offer participants an entry into thinking about the different strategies students use to solve the same problem, 192 – 40.

---

[7]For more information on minilessons, see Chapter 8, "Developing Efficient Computation with Minilessons," pp. 127–51 in *Young Mathematicians at Work: Constructing Number Sense, Addition, and Subtraction.*

- What are the students' strategies?
- How are they similar? How are they different?
- What do these strategies reveal about mathematical thinking (what big idea does a child need to have constructed in order to use such a strategy?)
- How does the teacher represent each strategy?

Clips 76 and 77 show Daniel and Domenica solving 192 – 40. In both clips, the students use constant difference to solve the problem, yet how they *play with the numbers* is very different. Because the way they change the problem is different, the similarities between the two strategies may elude participants.

FACILITATION TIP 8

One way to begin your work with participants is to have them solve the problems in the minilessons pages (in two different ways). Asking them to solve the problem in two ways allows them to use the algorithm, which, for some, may be their only strategy, and pushes them to think about other ways the given subtraction problem could be solved. As you discuss their strategies, post them on chart paper. Have them now think about the potential strategies third graders would use to solve these problems, and chart their ideas in a discussion. Keep both charts (participants' strategies and those they predicted third-grade students would use) posted. After they have had time to watch and analyze the clips, these charts can be returned to in a later discussion. Participants are usually surprised by the differences between their expectations of possible strategies and those that are actually used by students on the CD-ROM.

Daniel's Strategy

192–40

(100+92)–40

if   90–40=50,
then   92–40=52
add the 100 *back*
         100+52=152

Domenica's Strategy

192–40

+8 $\left(\quad\right)$ +8

200–48

200–48=152

Daniel's strategy is to split the 192 into two pieces; one piece (the 100) will be held onto and added back in and the other (92) will be used in subtraction.

Domenica uses constant difference. She knows that the difference between 200 and 48 is equal to the difference between 192 and 40.

192–40

+8 $\left(\quad\right)$ +8

200–48

Domenica's strategy is difficult for participants to understand. Often part of their confusion is connected to their puzzlement about *why she changed the numbers the way she did.* Many think she makes the problem more difficult with her strategy and they miss the fact that she has developed a big idea about subtraction: constant difference, $192 - 40 = (192 + 8) - (40 + 8)$.

One thing that will quickly surface to participants as they work through this page is their own understanding (or lack thereof) of subtraction. How can they begin to explore the meaning underlying student strategies if they have not developed some fundamental mathematical ideas themselves? If participants have never thought of subtraction as anything but removal and have used only the standard algorithm to solve subtraction problems, the students' strategies may be not only very surprising, but confusing as well. This will happen even if participants have highly developed *kid-watching* skills.

It is important then to develop participants' own understanding of subtraction as you work with the strings of problems in the minilessons. The work you do to deepen participants' content knowledge will support their ability to analyze the clips of the students.

The importance of developing computational efficiency (one of Michael's goals in doing mental math minilessons) and the connection this has to *looking to the numbers before picking a strategy*, can be brought up for discussion by juxtaposing Clips 79, 83, and 87. Where the students in Clips 83 and 87 use efficient strategies that are connected to the numbers in the problem, Daniel's strategy (Clip 79), which is similar to the splitting one he used in Clip 76, is difficult for him to use.

To solve the problem, 378 – 39, Daniel splits all the numbers, changing the problem into $(300 + 70 + 8) - (30 + 9)$. He works with the tens in the problem, and solves 70 – 30 = 40. He runs into trouble, however, with 8 – 9, and comes up with negative 1 only when a classmate corrects him (his original answer was 1). Next Daniel correctly subtracts 1 from 40 to get 39, but now becomes confused with what to do with the 39 and subtracts this from 300.

Some of his classmates correct Daniel and tell him that he should have added the 39 to the 300. One of them exhibits wonderful number sense when he wonders (and this pondering has nothing to do with the exact answer, but just with the reasonableness of Daniel's answer), "how could 378 minus 39 be 261?"

Daniel's splitting strategy confuses him; he has too many pieces and trying to remember what he should do with those pieces leads to problems (Should I add? Subtract? Where do all these pieces come from? How do I keep track of all the pieces?). This is also what makes the standard (subtraction) algorithm so difficult for children to understand. It is not only the place value.

Compare Daniel's struggle with the strategies shown in the other two clips. In Clip 87, Manuel uses constant difference and changes the problem 83 – 49 into 84 – 50. This is an efficient, elegant solution to the original problem. (Emmanuel, in Clip 89, succinctly explains why Manuel's strategy works: "You're adding one on to each number, so the difference is still the same.")

In Clip 83, Ian easily solves the problem 283 – 275 by counting up eight ("From 275 jump a five and then a three; the answer is eight"). Ian's strategy is

---

FACILITATION TIP 9

In the clips in "Minilessons": *Big Ideas for Subtraction,* students are seen working with a number of big ideas and strategies that you can use to highlight the distinction among subtraction models. To help participants understand the mathematical ideas behind students' strategies, you may want to spend time with participants exploring subtraction models.

For example, a subtraction problem, such as 93 – 69, can be thought of in a number of different ways:

- the distance, or difference, between 69 and 93 (missing addend 69 + ? = 93 or 93 – ? = 69)

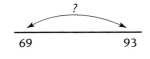

- the removal of 69 from 93

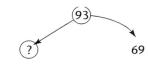

- a comparison between 69 and 93

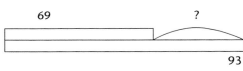

Since student strategies are connected to the big ideas they have constructed (or are constructing), a student who only understands one model of subtraction (the *take-away* model is the one most frequently presented by teachers and used in traditional word problems) is limited in *how he can solve a problem*. As a model, *removal* supports counting-back strategies, but this strategy is not always the most efficient way to solve a problem.

Consider two subtraction problems: 98 – 4 and 98 – 89. A counting-back strategy is a quick, efficient way to solve the first problem, but not the second. Since the *goal* of developing students' computational strategies *is efficiency,* the need for working with, and understanding, a variety of models is critical in bringing this about.

Although constructing the models for subtraction is important in the development of students' number sense, understanding the different models will not automatically translate into computational efficiency. This is where doing mental mathematics minilessons comes into play because it is here that students' strategies for solving problems are examined and discussed. Not only do these discussions develop students' repertoire of strategies, they also highlight what an efficient and elegant solution to a given problem looks like. As students consider what makes a strategy efficient, the idea of *looking to the numbers before picking a strategy* comes to the surface. This idea is a major component in the development of computationally efficient strategies and lies at the heart of number sense.

connected to the numbers—the closer they are on the number line, the more help-ful a counting-up strategy is. Michael represents Ian's strategy on the open number line, but asks him where his answer is, then when Ian says "It's right on the top," cir-cles the 5 + 3. This is an important question to ask because, depending on the strat-egy, the answer can be in a different place on the number line.

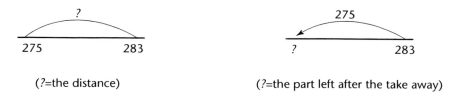

(*?=the distance*)   (*?=the part left after the take away*)

Another big idea students are constructing is *the connection between addition and subtraction*. In Clip 84, Ben explains this relationship to the class: "24 plus 31 = 55 is the same problem as 55 minus 31 = 24, right?"

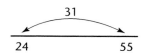

Clip 84, Michael's representation of Ben's statement about the connection between addition and subtraction

Backburner

◉ *This is the last page in the folder "Minilessons." However, you may have other ques-tions on this topic that you would like to investigate. Go to the TOOLS menu above and add them to your backburner notes.*

See *Backburner* notes, page 5.

GAMES

Games

◉ *In this folder you can investigate several games and the potential mathematical ideas and strategies kindergarteners and first graders use and struggle to construct.*

Understanding what mathematical ideas are embedded in the structure of the game may allay participants' uncertainties about the effectiveness of games. The CD-ROM question is asking participants to analyze the games to the big ideas and what children's potential strategies might be—and thus may make this task meaningful and clear. Par-ticipants may come to appreciate how the questions and comments the teachers make as the game is played are an important piece of the teaching/learning dynamic. An-other important piece in this dynamic is how teachers' understanding of children's comprehension is the determining factor in supporting and challenging children to de-velop more efficient strategies. This is what can happen with the use of games.[8]

---

[8]Refer participants to *Young Mathematicians at Work: Constructing Number Sense, Addition, and Subtraction*, Chapter 3 "Number Sense on the Horizon," pp. 37–41, "Using Games."

First-grade teacher Kathy Sillman has organized the playing of games into a workshop time for the whole class. Different games are set up at different tables, and children have been paired to play them. The games are played cooperatively because the objective is for pairs to discuss and share ideas and to agree upon a course of action.

Kathy walks from group to group and joins them to listen in on what the children are saying, to watch what they are doing, and to ask questions based on these observations that may engender disequilibrium or stretch children's thinking.

What follows are brief analyses of the mathematical ideas embedded in the three games, *Capture Ten*, *Compare*, and *Racing Dice*. (See Appendix B for fuller descriptions of the game boards and the materials that accompany these teacher-made games.)

In *Capture Ten*, children determine the sum of two number cards (e.g., 8 and 7) and use the sum to figure out how the cards can be placed in pockets on a game board labeled 10 + 1, 10 + 2 . . . 10 + 9, 20. What big ideas in early number must students have constructed in order to understand that 8 + 7 = 15 = 10 + 5? Conservation is one such idea (no matter how a number is arranged the total is the same); hierarchical inclusion is another idea (the nesting of small numbers within the largest one); part-whole relationships (the whole does not change even as the parts are rearranged); and compensation. But the game is primarily designed to support the development of the "making of tens" strategy, which is an important strategy for addition.

Compare is a game based on a big idea in early number, magnitude *(Which is more?)*. But unlike the childhood game of War, (TERC's *Compare*), this Mathematics in the City (MitC) version adds an additional dimension. It is designed with a context to support the big idea of hierarchical inclusion (the nesting of the smaller numbers that are inside a larger number) and part-whole relations. The game board has pockets labeled 0 through 10. The child whose number is more than her partner's puts *both* cards in that pocket, (e.g., 10 is more than 7, so both 10 and 7 are placed in the 10 pocket). When the game is over and it is time to empty the pockets, the teacher joins the children and asks, "What cards do you think will be inside this [8] pocket?" Some children may say "8" and will be very surprised to see that other numbers besides 8 are inside and that all of them are less than 8. "Why do you think those cards are in here, too?" is a question whose answers give the teacher indications of children's understandings and confusions about hierarchical inclusion.

In *Racing Dice*, each player, in turn, rolls two dice, determines what the sum is, and writes the sum on the game board. Dice games support individual children's strategies at the same that time they support the development of other strategies and big ideas.

How will the children determine the sum of the pips on the dice? Participants may say that

- some children may count the pips on one die, count the pips on the other die, and then go back to figure out how many;
- some may recognize the number pattern on one die and count on by ones from the other die;
- some may start with the die that has more pips and count on the pips from the other die;
- some children may know the sum of a double, if one is thrown.

FACILITATION TIP 10

In this CD-ROM section on *Games,* participants will be asked the repeating question, *What mathematical ideas, strategies, and struggles do you expect to see as children play these games?* Before participants read that multilayered question, it is important to ask them to examine their perceptions of what games do. You may find, for example, that many believe that games are respites from "real" work or that they help children discover new learning. If participants keep to such beliefs, the mathematics potentials that games hold may not immediately be obvious to them, and the question above may be mystifying. Moreover, although the games are structured, the play is open-ended, that is, children playing at their individual levels of understanding might say and do the unexpected. This can cause disequilibrium in new teachers as well as in teachers new to using games in their classrooms. The purpose in playing games—for teachers to observe and question children's ideas and strategies as they reveal them in their play—also may be disconcerting to new teachers, who may not know what to say or do and thus feel that they have lost control of the teaching.

Students' ideas of cardinality and strategies of counting and adding can come into play: subitizing the amount on one die (or on both dice) then counting on from the other die; counting three times (the first die, the second die, and then all the pips on both dice); starting with the bigger number and counting on (the commutative property supports this strategy); knowing sums of doubles; knowing particular sums; and so on. To challenge the children, a teacher can substitute a numeral die for a die with pips to support the development of "counting on." The game is still played with two dice, but one has pips, the other, numerals.

Kathy's teacher-made game board has a base line under which the numbers 2 through 12 are written across in each square. In the squares above the base-line numbers, she has lightly written the numerals in dashes. When a child rolls the dice and determines the sum of the pips, he traces over the numeral of the sum in the box just above the number. When all the boxes in the column above a number are filled, the game ends.

Capture Ten

◉ *Two first-grade students are playing* Capture Ten *with Madeline Chang. Each turns over a card. Together they try to determine the sum of the two cards and put these cards in the correct pocket. The pockets are labeled: 10 + 1; 10 + 2; . . . .What mathematical ideas and strategies do the children use as they set to work?*

Capture Ten is another MitC game designed to support the development of making a tens strategy for addition, for example, $8 + 5 = 10 + 3$. It has 3 rows of pockets glued to it, labeled as follows. Top row: $10 + 0 \ldots 10 + 3$; middle row: $10 + 4 \ldots 10 + 7$; and the bottom row: $10 + 8$, $10 + 9$, 20.

One deck of cards has numerals on them; the other are the TERC number cards found in *Investigations in Number, Data, and Space*. These cards—in addition to having the numeral on them —show pictures of birds, flowers, and so on, arranged in groupings of 5s. For example, this is how 6 is arranged :

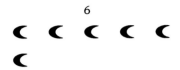

The cards are dealt so that the players have stacks of cards equal to each other. Players play cooperatively to share ideas and determine their strategies. When playing, a *rekenrek* is used for children to prove their choice of pocket. (The 10 + 10 structure of the *rekenrek* is ideally suited to be used in this way.)

This game has two challenges: the first is for the two players to find the sum of the numbers on the two cards; the second is to 'capture the ten' in that sum and figure out how many leftovers there are. Then they place the cards into the appropriate pocket (10 + 0, 10 + 1, etc.). For example, if they turn over a 9 and a 6, they place the cards in 10 + 5.

How might the first graders do this? Plan to have a discussion with the participants to brainstorm children's possible ideas, struggles, and strategies. For adding strategies, participants may anticipate that first graders

- may start with the number card and count on the pictures from the other card;
- will know the doubles that turn up;
- will know some sums without counting, etc.

Some participants may say that placing the cards (e.g., 9 + 6) into the appropriate pocket is too hard for first graders to do; others may opine that students will examine the sum, capture the ten, and then count how many are left over; they may say that some children, like Willie in the minilesson *Playing Tag*, will decompose the 6 into 5 and 1, then add 1 to 9 to make 10.

Clip 29 shows another strategy. The boys have turned over 8 and 7 and say "15" right away. The teacher, Madeline Chang, asks the important question, "How did you know that?" The boy in the striped shirt says that 8 + 7 will be one less than the sum that they had previously determined (9 + 7 = 16) "because 8 is one less than 9." He does not add 8 + 7 because he has noticed that 7 is one of the addends in both 8 + 7 and 9 + 7. His strategy is to compare the 9 and the 8. Because 8 is one less than 9, he reasons that 8 + 7 will be one less than 9 + 7, or 15.

Compare

⊚ *Two first graders in Kathy Sillman's class are playing* Compare. *Each turns over a card and they compare them. They decide which is more, and put both of them in a pocket with a label equal to the highest amount. The children seem to have an easy time comparing 2 and 8. Why do you think that is?*

  Describe the mathematical ideas and strategies the students use as they set to work. What mathematical ideas might this game develop?

In the play that participants view in Clip 28, because the boy with the 8 has the higher number, he takes the 2 and puts both cards in the 8 pocket. Both boys agree that 8 is bigger than 2. As participants in their small groups watch this clip, they can spend some time responding to the question, *Why do you think that the children seem to have an easy time comparing 2 and 8?* This is a nice clip to use to have a discussion on subitizing.

◎ *Two other first graders are playing* Racing Dice. *They throw two dice, determine the sum, and mark that number on a racing dice chart. What mathematical ideas and counting strategies do the children use?*

In Clips 22 and 24 through 27 Tafarii and Mary Claire are playing *Racing Dice*. Tafarii rolls a double 6, but she uses a counting-on strategy. She puts the dice together and reads the one on the left first "6," then from the right die counts on, 7, 8, 9, 10, 11, 12.

FACILITATION TIP 11

➚ *Racing Dice.* Ask participants to suppose they are Kathy Sillman and are watching the girls play the game. They have noticed that Tafarii and Mary Claire use the same strategy—they subitize the pips on one of the dice and count on the pips from the second die—whether or not the first die has the fewest pips or the most pips. The girls appear to do this easily, but their strategy can lead to counting errors.

In groups, have participants think of a *constraint* what might inhibit their counting habit—to stretch the girls' counting strategies. For example, instead of supplying two dice that have pips, one such constraint might be to substitute one of the dice with pips for one that has numerals 1–6 on it, etc.

Mary Claire rolls a 2 and a 5. She reads the die closest to her first, says, "2," and then counts on from the other die, "3, 4, 5, 6, 7," and traces over a 7. Most likely she has not yet constructed the big idea of the commutative property of addition. She counts on, but from the smaller number.

The Shoe Game in Kindergarten

◎ *Two kindergarten children in Shanna Schwartz's class are playing* The Shoe Game. *The track on the game board is made of pairs of shoes. Alternately, they throw a die and turn a second die to match it. They determine the total number of pips on both dice and move that number of shoes. What are these students constructing mathematically?*

At play in *The Shoe Game* (developed by Madeline Chang) is the development of several big ideas.[9] As seen in the clips, the kindergartners use very beginning strategies, from counting all the pips on the dice by ones (ignoring the double) to using just one die to mentally construct the double. Also underpinning *The Shoe Game* is the connection between counting by *pairs* of shoes or by the *shoes* themselves. The big idea of unitizing is inherent in this game: understanding that one pair of shoes are two shoes (one 2 is two 1s) and that two shoes are one pair (two 1s are one 2). The commutative property of multiplication may also come up for discussion, $2 \times 5 = 5 \times 2$. On the die is 5 and it is doubled to move 10. But children also begin to notice with interest that this is five pairs of shoes, too.

---

[9]Refer participants to p. 101 in *Young Mathematicians at Work: Constructing Number Sense, Addition, and Subtraction*. It describes investigations of first graders on doubles and on what comes in pairs. From these investigations, a *Double Your Number* game was devised. *The Shoe Game* game board evolved from that game.

The Shoe Game game board shows pairs of shoes moving along a curving path. The two dice used in this game are of different colors. The players roll one die, and then, using the die of the other color, match its number to make a double. The game piece is then moved that number of shoes (or that number of pairs).

In Clip 1, boy 1 has rolled a 6, looks at it and says "6" without counting. As he makes the other die read 6, his partner says, "You go 12." Boy 1 shakes his head, and even though he has just said "6" from the die he rolled, he now counts it: "1, 2 . . . 6," and then counts on the pips from the second die. In so doing, he miscounts, "7, 8, 9, 11, 12, 14." His partner stops him and counts both dice by ones to 12. Boy 1 shakes his head, but begins to move his marker. This interaction between the boys is interesting in that it shows that learning cannot be transmitted from one person to another, especially when the one who doesn't know is in the midst of puzzling things out. In this case, the directions from his partner, instead of being helpful, cause boy 1 to revert to a less efficient strategy (e.g., when he first rolled the dice, he had subitized 6; after the interruption, he starts from 1).

In Clip 2, two other children are playing the game. Their teacher, Shanna Schwartz, intervenes to highlight for one player what his partner has just done. (The girl rolled one die—a 5—and does not match a second die and add another 5 for a total of 10, but instead moves by five *pairs*, ending at a tenth shoe.) Shanna demonstrates the girl's unitizing strategy of counting by pairs to her partner and uses two fingers to indicate each pair on the game board:

Shanna: 1 pair of shoes; 2 pairs of shoes, 3 pairs of shoes; 4 pairs of shoes; 5 pairs of shoes *(landing on the tenth shoe)*. So she rolled a 5 and she moved 5 pairs of shoes!

Boy: Yeah!

Shanna: Will that always happen? (a good question to explore the commutative property; in this case the generalization about doubles and pairs)

Boy: Sometimes.   (a telling answer because he has not yet understood the connection between two fives and five twos.

Backburner

◎ *This is the last page in the folder "Games." However, you may have other questions on this topic that you would like to investigate. Go to the TOOLS menu above and add them to your backburner notes.*

See *Backburner* notes, page 5.

INVESTIGATIONS

Taking Inventory: Blocks

◎ *In the following clips from Jodi Weisbart's K–1 classroom, three children—Noah, Declan, and Gabrielle—are taking inventory of the blocks in the block area. What mathematical ideas and strategies do the children use as they set to work? What mathematical ideas are they developing?*

In Clip 30, Noah is taking the blocks off the shelf and counting each block he removes. His actions (tagging, or in this case, taking) are in synchrony with his voice as he counts. His careful removal of the blocks can be seen as a form of organization (he systematically takes them off by depleting one column before moving on to the next).

Noah struggles with *the social knowledge of counting—knowing the labels for what he is counting*. In two separate instances he is seen asking his peers what comes next ("I don't even know what comes after twenty-eight; What comes after fifty-nine? One hundred?") There is a difference between these two questions mathematically. Knowing what comes after twenty-eight is related to the repeating sequence of one to nine between the decades; knowing the name of the next decade is the repeating sequence of the tens. Noah is struggling with these, which gives us insight into his understanding of our number system.

He also mislabels one of the blocks as he counts, saying sixteen instead of fifteen. When another child corrects him, he renames the block he has counted, and continues without missing a beat. There is a big mathematical idea that underlies his actions as he counts—for every object counted there is a name. Yet knowing the name for what comes next, the singsong of counting, social knowledge, *is not necessarily connected to being able to count to accurately answer the question, How many?*[10] Notice how Noah stops counting to get the name for what comes next and continues to count once he obtains it—he has a conversation about what comes after twenty-eight, yet is able to continue counting from twenty-nine.

In order to do this, Noah has to be able to hold on to the previous quantity in his head. Underlying his counting-on strategy is a big idea—cardinality—the last number counted names *all* the objects within the set, not the last object. Compare Noah's ability to pick up from where he was with Declan in Clip 31, who loses count when Noah needs help and asks questions. To answer him, Declan's own block count is interrupted, and he has to recount his blocks from one.

Counting by Ones. Noah and Declan have been counting their blocks by ones. (There are a number of clips across the inventory pages that illustrate children counting by ones, Clips 30, 31 on this page, and Clips 38, 39, 40, 43, Snap Cubes.)

Counting large quantities of objects poses several challenges for the K–1 students. They must not only figure out how to count the objects, but also how to keep track of what is counted so that they can record and report this information to the

FACILITATION TIP 12

The dialogue provided in Appendix D: Dialogue Box D: Taking Inventory, is evidence of an interactive learning environment in which the facilitator works to develop a number of critical ideas simultaneously. At the same time that she is working to develop participants' kid watching, she also is starting to build a community of learners. This is done by valuing each participants' thoughts—note the initial recording of each participants' ideas without commenting on what they are saying. The facilitator also stresses the importance of communication between participants, emphasizing it as the foundation of their working together in small groups (see suggestions provided by the facilitator for their small-group work).

The facilitator also works to sharpen participants' powers of observation, one of the primary goals of a beginning journey. She

- **controls the flow of the conversation** (it does not jump all over the place). This is done by asking the participants after a first viewing to state their observations, but not to comment on each other's ideas;
- **sets the parameters for kid watching.** This is done slowly and subtly; a list of rules is *not given to participants at the outset, but evolves from the contradictions and interpretations that arise from the different stories they tell and the need for accurate retelling;*
- **develops participants' kid watching.** This is done by asking participants for supporting evidence for their interpretations and observations as they set off to work in pairs.

The facilitator uses the technology as a tool to

- **deepen thinking.** The repeated viewing of the clips helps participants refine their thinking and reflect on the ideas of others. The level of accuracy in their stories improves as the facilitator pushes participants toward a more precise retelling. At the end of the discussion, participants are sent back to work in pairs, expected to use some of the kid-watching tools they have just developed. Witness the use of cycles of observing, discussing, analyzing, reflecting, developing narrative knowledge, and expanding personal repertoires and generalizing.
- **work with the range of learners in the class, and provide experiences broad enough to meet different needs.** Some participants will need to spend more time than others to develop nonjudgmental ways of looking at students. For participants who quickly develop their powers of observation, another kind of journey is more appropriate, one in which they begin to think about the mathematical ideas that underlie students' actions (strategies) and words.

---

[10]For an example of this go to the folder, *Seven Candies in a Tin*. In Clip 48, Shatisha, when asked how many candies are in a tin that she has just counted, recounts. The candies are in the tin and cannot be manipulated, but she counts anyway. For her, the question How many? means to recite the singsong and is not necessarily connected to the quantity of the objects being counted.

entire class. If they count the objects by ones, there are many opportunities to lose count.

Because taking inventory is a truly problematic situation, students grapple with two important ideas: *Are there ways to organize their materials to make counting easier? What are more efficient ways of counting large quantities of objects?*

Participants may comment that although organizing the materials is a strategy that helps in counting, it may not necessarily mean it will move students beyond counting by ones. What, then, is the connection between creating a structure (e.g., grouping materials in fives or tens) and using that structure to think with? To answer this, participants must think about several other critical questions including

- What mathematical ideas must a student construct in order to move beyond counting by ones?
- What are the important landmarks in this journey, and how can they be recognized in a student's actions and words?

One way to help participants reflect on the development of counting strategies is to use Clips 42, 44, and 45 and analyze them in terms of student growth and development. While these clips are very brief, rich detail can be mined from each of them. To focus their analysis, use the following questions: What are the students' strategies? How do these change over time? What (if anything) supports these changes?

Counting in Groups.   Initially, Declan was working in tandem with Noah (Clips 30 and 31), and counting the blocks by ones. Glimpsed in the sequence of short Clips 42, 44, and 45, Declan and Gabrielle are seen developing a strategy to count that requires them to use groups of blocks—now bound in groups of five with rubber bands. While on the surface the question remains the same (How many blocks?), their organization of these blocks into groups of five creates a problematic situation: What is it that they are counting and how are they to count these groups?

In Clip 42, Jodi, their teacher, highlights their struggles when she asks, "5 and 5 makes 10, and 5 more makes . . . ?" Declan reverts to counting the blocks by ones. Gabrielle's response, "We can do it easier," reflects an understanding that counting the groups *is a faster and easier way to count.* But the question still remains, What is it we are counting and how do we count it?

Gabrielle touches each group of five and says, "10, 30, 40, 50, 60, 70, 80, 90, 100, 1000." She knows each group needs a name, but struggles with more than knowing the singsong of skip counting by tens. When, at a whole-class meeting, Gabrielle and Declan share how they count their banded fives, their understanding of counting by groups is shakily evolving. Declan covers two fives with his hand (there are three sets of 2-fives), as he counts 10, 20, 30. But immediately he says, "No," and Gabrielle steps in and counts each five by ten: "10, 20, 30 . . . 60." Is it 30? Is it 60?" Declan tries again and counts to 40! (he counts the first 2 groups of five (10), next five (20), next five (30) and the last two-fives (40). Underlying the children's struggles in Clips 42 and 44 is a big idea, that when you skip count you are counting by the amount in the group and the total of your count is increasing by that quantity. What we are counting—the amount in the group—affects the name we say.

In Clip 45, Gabrielle's development of this skip-counting idea is reflected in her actions and words. Touching each group of five within the grouping of ten, she counts, saying, " . . . 5 and 5, 10; 5 and 5, 20; 5 and 5, 30." Over the course of three clips, Gabrielle has developed a skip-counting strategy, constructing an understanding that what she counts by is what is in the groups she is counting. This is a huge developmental shift on the landscape of learning.

Taking Inventory: Snap Cubes

◎ *In the same K–1 classroom, Donna, Amanda, and Alicia are taking inventory of the multilink and snap cubes. What mathematical ideas and strategies are they using? Describe their organization. What mathematical struggles do they have?*

Donna, like Noah, counts by ones. Although she has snapped her cubes together, she touches individual cubes as she counts. At first glance it would seem that she has organized by number, but a closer look shows that her organization is by color (Clip 38). She counts the cubes by ones and indicates by the sigh in her voice when she reaches one hundred (Clip 40) that she has reached a milestone.

Compared to Noah's struggles counting blocks, Amanda (Clip 39) knows the counting sequence (she does not struggle with what number name comes next), but she miscounts the cubes. She, too, counts by ones, although she has snapped the cubes in groups of ten. Careful watching of her actions in conjunction with her voice shows that initially her tagging is not in synchrony with her count as she touches the cubes. That she miscounts also becomes apparent when one notices that, at the end of a group of ten, she says sixty-nine instead of seventy.

Children's struggles with what comes next in the counting sequence are not uniform. For example, in Clip 43, Alicia, like Noah, also has constructed cardinality, and struggles with what comes next. There is an important distinction between their struggles, however. Where Noah's counting breaks down in different places (e.g., 15, 28, 59), Alicia struggles at the decade—"What comes after 29, 39, and 49?" Her consistent pausing at each decade reflects a struggle to know the name that breaks the pattern of the count. (That young children struggle with the logic [or lack thereof!] in our base-ten counting sequence is often reflected in the names they give these numbers, twenty-ten for thirty, thirty-ten for forty, etc.)

The distinction between Noah's and Alicia's struggles may not be immediately apparent to participants who are developing kid watching. One way to focus their observations is to ask them if they can imitate Alicia's counting. To do this, they must consider her actions in conjunction with her words. For example, as she struggles with what comes after 29, Alicia holds her two fingers on the 29th and 30th cubes. When she loses count, she goes back to recount the third group of ten. Before she does this, she places her hand over two stacks of ten and says, "20." This action occurs again (where she miscounts from 20, 21, 22, 23 . . . 29, 50, 51, saying "50, 51" at the 29th and 30th cubes. She goes back to recount, places her hand over the three groups of ten, says, "30" and counts on, "31, 32, 33 . . .") an indication that Alicia is using the groups of ten as reference points in her counting.

These are important details to bring up in a discussion with participants because underlying Alicia's action is the construction of the idea that two groups of ten are twenty and three groups of ten are thirty. *Unitizing*, the ability to think of a group as the unit and using this unit to count, is a big idea on the landscape of learning for early number.

Taking Inventory: Paper Bags

◉ *Two other children, Isa and Eli, are also taking inventory. They try to find out how many bags there are. Compare their work with that of Donna, Amanda, and Alicia counting the cubes.*

Isa and Eli have bundled their bags in packs of ten and have painstakingly counted each pack to make certain each contains exactly ten bags. They know that if they are to skip count by ten, there must be ten in each group.

Together in Clip 34, Isa and Eli are counting: ". . . 170, 180, 190, 200, 201, 202 . . . " A sound from Jodi alerts them to stop and remember that they are counting by tens. Eli says, "210" (Isa considers this and then nods) and they continue ". . . 220, 230, 240." Eli says, "240 bags!" Isa reminds him that there are 9 loose ones to count in and tells him, "249."

Knowing what comes after each hundred is quite difficult. Children often think that 200 comes after 100, for example. Others commonly switch to ones beyond the hundred mark, like Isa and Eli in this clip and Amanda in Clip 37.

Amanda is now counting her towers of ten by ten: " . . . 60, 70, 80, 90, 100, 101, 102." Bryan, her partner, tells her, "That's not 102. Those are two *tens*; it's 120."

Taking Inventory: Representing the Amounts

◎ *As the children in the K–1 class are continuing their inventory investigation they find ways to represent the amounts. What different ways do they use? What do their representations tell you about their mathematical development?*

Clips 32, 33, and 41 offer participants an opportunity to think about how written notation develops for learners. That notation *develops* at all may be surprising to some participants! They may never have considered that counting and writing a number to represent what is counted are not concurrent developments, and that children's informal recordings can go through different stages (e.g., the difference between pictorial, iconic, and numeric representations of quantity).[11]

Before sending them off to watch and analyze the clips, it might be helpful to explore participants' understanding of written notation and its development in a whole-group discussion. They have spent time working through the CD-ROM analyzing children's counting strategies in various contexts where the overarching question has been, *What does a child need to know in order to answer the question, how many?* Reshaping this question (e.g., What does a child need to know in order to record the twenty-seven objects they have counted with the numeral 27?) will bring participants' ideas about notation to the surface. Their answers, which could range from behaviorist observations (they need to practice writing the numbers to know how to write them) to more developmental ones (children's writing is connected to the maturation of their fine motor skills), will probably *not* take into account that students can be *taught* to write numbers, but have little understanding of what those numbers actually mean. What is equally important to bring up in a discussion as they watch the clips—perhaps a radical idea for some—is the notion that *if students are allowed to develop their own notations, their informal representations will be reflections of the mathematical ideas they are developing.*

In Clips 32 and 33, Declan, Noah, and Shawnee are recording what they have counted onto one recording sheet. Their recordings differ in a number of ways and analyzing these can offer participants insights into students' struggles with, and the development of, notation.

Shawnee's recording of 15.

Delcan's recording of 27. Note how he labels the number with a drawing of the kind of block counted.

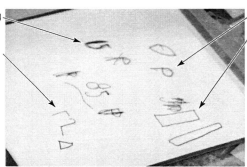

Noah's recording of 9

Declan draws two blocks to represent the two blocks he has counted. He has crossed out the number 3 to the left of his drawing.

As Noah calls out, "There are 15," Shawnee is already writing a 5 on the recording sheet. She sits back, looks at what she has written, and then puts the numeral 1 to the left of the 5, making the number 15.

As she is doing this, Declan is drawing two blocks, and says, "You can even draw it!" What he draws becomes the subject of conversation as Shawnee points to the two blocks he's drawn, and says, "That's 10—no, that's 11." Declan's puzzlement—he is not thinking of what he has written as a number—is reflected in his question to Shawnee, "That's 11?" He then points to the blocks he has drawn, and counts, "1, 2." To offer further explanation of what his representation means, Declan states, "Well,

---

[11]For a more in-depth discussion of this, refer to Chapter 4, "Place Value on the Horizon," in the companion book, *Young Mathematicians at Work: Constructing Number Sense, Addition, and Subtraction.*

I don't need to write a 2 because you can draw what there is in here [i.e., draw a picture of what he has just counted]."

Shawnee's confusion about what his drawing represents can be used as an entry into a discussion about how children's ideas about notation develop. While the question, "Why does Declan draw the blocks?" cannot be answered definitively, one hypothesis participants might propose is that perhaps he does not know how to write a 2.[12] Clip 33 can be used as evidence of this hypothesis: Declan writes the number twenty-seven, albeit incorrectly, and queries his group-mates, "Is that how you write a two?"

But in Clips 32 and 33 there are other, more important ideas than whether or not Declan can remember how to write numerals. At the heart of Declan's recordings are two ideas: (1) the number he is writing stands for a quantity; and (2) this amount also can be represented by drawing the actual objects. But what shifts Declan's strategy from pictorial to symbolic representation?

This is not a question that is easily answered, but it is one that participants need to think about if they are to understand some factors that influence the development of student representations. As they reflect on *what might be influencing Declan's changing representations*, be sure to have them support what they are saying with evidence from the video clips.

Whatever participants' ideas, there are some critical questions to ask:

- Why might a student's representational strategies be different for two and twenty-seven?

- What is the role of context (counting large quantities and representing) and how does it scaffold development? How does the context nudge children toward more efficient forms of notation?

- What role does social interaction play in the development of student strategies?

Declan is a powerful example to use in this discussion because participants have already examined the evolution of his counting strategies (see Clips 42, 44, and 45). When confronted with counting large amounts of objects, his strategy shifted from counting by ones to organizing and grouping the blocks in fives. When presented with another truly problematic situation—how to show the twenty-seven blocks that he has counted—Declan's strategy for representing that quantity changes. Could it be that two blocks are easy to draw, but drawing twenty-seven blocks in this way is tedious? Could Declan's shifting representation also be connected to the fact that his group is recording *their* totals onto *one* sheet, and that the need for being understood— how you communicate your ideas and what are socially acceptable ways of representing them—becomes an issue for him?

Whatever the answer—and it may be multifaceted—it is clear that Declan is struggling to develop a system of notation that represents what he has counted and that also communicates that quantity to others. That these ideas are developing simultaneously is evidenced in Clip 33. This entire clip is an interesting example of group dynamics and how *meaning is negotiated by students through puzzlement, discussion, and even disagreement.*

In Declan's writing of the number 27, Shawnee recognizes that he has not only made a backward 7, but has also written the number incorrectly (ᒥ2). Twice she says to him, "No, it's twenty . . . seven." Her voice emphasizes and lengthens the word, *twenty*, to indicate its importance. She also uses her pen to point to the 20 in 27 by first tapping the 2 in the number Declan has written and then indicating, by putting her pen to the left of the 7, where the 20—the 2—should go. This notation becomes hotly debated within the trio of students, with Noah offering the olive branch to Declan,

---

[12]It might be helpful here to have participants relook at the research of Martin Hughes described in Chapter 4 of *Young Mathematicians at Work: Constructing Number Sense, Addition, and Subtraction.*

who has become increasingly defensive about his notation, when Noah says to him, "You're good; you're really good."

That students are developing notation is apparent in Clips 32 and 33. It is important to remember that while participants can delineate what students are doing, they may do this without thinking about *why these struggles occur*. To help them consider this question and go deeper into the meaning behind the strategies, ask them to think about what mathematical ideas underpin students' struggles with notation. At the heart of this discussion are some big ideas on the landscape of learning for early number.

Clip 41 can be used to probe the mathematical ideas behind children's struggles. Here Amanda is seen recording the number of cubes she has counted on an index card. (Although Amanda does not count in this clip; she is seen counting in Clips 37 and 39. There are twelve groups of ten that she has counted.) The number she writes is not clear, but the motion of her hand indicates she has written a five-digit number on the index card—10020—to represent the cubes counted. Her partner recognizes that she has written the number incorrectly and says, pointing to it, "No, not that!" So why does Amanda write 120 as 10020? Is there something more at play here than not remembering how the numbers look?

Shawnee's language is similar to Amanda's writing 10020 for 120. "Twenty . . . seven," Shawnee keeps insisting, "It's 20 . . . 7." What does this language and recording reflect about student thinking? What is the difference in notation between 10020 and 120 in terms of a child's mathematical development?

At the heart of this discussion is the difference between additive and multiplicative systems of notation. Our way of recording numbers reflects a multiplicative system in which there are only nine digits, and what a digit means is determined by its place in the number system. To notate one-hundred-twenty as 120 means that the 1 means one group of 100, the 2 means two groups of ten, and the 0 means no units.

This big idea—unitizing—is at the heart of the packing investigation the children have been exploring! Difficulties with unitizing are reflected in students' struggles with notation, as well as in their counting. These struggles and the insights children gain from their puzzlements are highlighted in Clips 36, 94, and 212 on the next page in the folder.

Taking Inventory, Continued

◉ *Observe the K–1 students working in the following video clips. What ideas are they constructing?*

In Clip 36, Isa and Eli have grouped their bags in tens and have used this structure to figure out how many bags they have. (To figure out the total number of bags, they skip counted the packs by ten and then added on the extras ones [the loose bags].) When Jodi asks them, "How many packs do you have?" the answer—contained in the total number of bags they have just figured out—is not immediately apparent to Isa and Eli, and they begin to recount the packs (one pack, two packs, etc.)! Place value for them is still on the horizon.

Later (Clip 94), the entire class is seated in the meeting area for a discussion around the numbers on a chart, which has been structured by Jodi to bring place value ideas up for discussion (note the columns labeled: total number of objects, packs, loose). Isa has noticed a pattern in the numbers recorded on the chart paper and shares her idea with the class: "The number to the left [in a number] means the number of packs and this number [the one on the right] is the loose ones [or the ones that could not be packed in a group of 10]." This is a big idea for children to develop and a significant landmark on the landscape of early number. Even after the children have packed their objects in groups of ten, discussed their findings, and listened to other children's insights into this pattern (e.g., Isa's noticing), place value is still "under construction" for many.

The children continue to report their inventory counts, which Jodi records on another chart labeled: Item, Total, Packs, Loose. Many counts have been recorded

Item	Total	Packs	Loose
Paper Bags	249	24	9
Snap Cubes	64	6	4
Books	17	1	7
Books	23	2	3

when Cosmo (Clip 214) says, "The board! Look! 23!" His noticing of a pattern in the numbers galvanizes the group, who excitedly say, "Yes. 17 and 51! 52! and 64!" Jodi asks, "Are you noticing something?"

The children are excited as they notice the pattern of repeating numerals. But do they understand why the pattern works?

Strips for the Art Show: Measurements

◉ *In the following clips children from Hildy Martin's second grade are measuring the sides of different pieces of paper. They measure each side with multilink cubes. What mathematical ideas and strategies do the children use as they set to work? What mathematical struggles do they have?*

The clips in *Strips for the Art Show* are a window into the counting and grouping strategies used by second graders as they measure the long and short sides of a variety of papers of different sizes and colors. As participants analyze these clips, they will need to think about the similarities and differences in students' counting and organizational strategies and what these reveal about their mathematical development.

Although some of these clips are short in duration, there is a wealth of detail for participants to consider. In several of the clips (59, 63, and 65), the subtleties of student actions alone need to be clearly distinguished before participants can think about the mathematical meaning behind their strategies.

Some questions to help focus participants in their video viewing:

- How do students group the multilink cubes? Does this grouping affect/support their counting strategy? If so, how?
- What strategies do students use to obtain their measurements?
- Can you imitate a student's strategy? What thinking might underlie this strategy?
- Do students' strategies change? If so, how? What affects the change?
- How are student strategies similar and/or different?
- What mathematical ideas underlie their strategies?
- What difficulties do students encounter? How do these struggles affect their counting?

The student strategies fall into three broad categories:

- counting by ones (Clips 57 and 65);
- skip counting by tens (Clips 58, 59, 60, and 64); and
- marking groups and unitizing (Clip 63).

These categories are broad because a number of student pairs use more than one strategy to obtain a measurement (e.g., in Clip 64, Lilly and Melissa count by ones and skip count by tens).

Counting by Ones. There are many instances of children obtaining their measurements by counting the cubes by ones (Clips 57, 59, 60, 64, and 65). It is important, however, for participants to recognize that while some of these children *only* count their cubes by ones (Clips 57, 60, and 65), there are other clues to student thinking that also need to be considered in any discussion of student strategies.

One key feature in a discussion about clues to student thinking needs to be *how students organize their materials*. When viewed from this perspective, there is only one group who counts by ones that has no clearly discernible color organization. Anthony and Sarah, in Clip 57, use two colors of cubes, but these are not organized in a way that would support counting in groups.

In Clips 60 and 65, both groups of students have organized their materials in a way to support counting. While Lindsey and Lucero in Clip 60 have their Multi-links grouped in a repeating pattern of ten (ten red, ten green, etc.), the clip only shows them counting the units (31, 32, 33, 34); it is not clear *how* they have counted (if they counted the preceding cubes by tens or ones). That their count is off, however, is obvious: their row of multilinks has four groups of ten and four units. It is clear that the clipboard Lindsey holds covers one group of ten—the ten they are missing in their final measurement.

In Clip 65, Angelica and Diana have organized their multilinks into groups of ten, which are subdivided into five red and five green. Though stacks of *ten* have been prebuilt, Angelica begins to measure the paper with one group of five green. Diana hands her a stack of ten (five red and five green), which Angelica connects to the five green placed along the length of the paper she is measuring. Angelica then reaches for another stack of ten. When it does not fit (because the multilinks cannot be joined), she flips the cubes and creates a group of ten (green). This breaks the pattern of fives that is clearly discernible in the beginning of her measurement. It is important to note that Angelica counts the cubes by ones even though the beginning of her multilinks row could have been counted by fives or tens.

Skip Counting Strategies. In Clips 59 and 64, students have multiple strategies for obtaining measurements. While they organize their cubes in groups and use this to count, they also recount their measurements by ones. It is important for participants to consider what is affecting the change in their counting strategies. In order to be able to do this, participants must focus on very specific details in each of the clips.

In Clip 58, Shannon counts his multilinks, which are grouped in an alternating pattern of five pink and five yellow, by tens. His physical action as he counts (he places his hand on both groups as he counts, "10, 20, 30"), clearly shows that he is thinking of the two groups of five as a ten.

Andrew and Shannon in Clip 59 are measuring a different piece of paper. When Shannon begins to count the cubes by ones, Andrew stops him and counts by tens, "10, 20, 30." The problem here is that the cubes are organized with the repeating pattern of fives, but there is a slight change—a single cube has been added before the first group of five. This alters the structure of the pattern into $1 + (5 + 5) + (5 + 5) + 5$.

Shannon indicates the single yellow cube that Andrew omitted in his count, and recounts, "10, 20, 30, 31." There is some disagreement between the two boys about the measurement and Shannon resolves the situation by recounting the cubes by ones. Now he gets 26. His statement at the end of this count, "26—how can that be?" reflects his disequilibrium—he recognizes that he has just counted the same stack of cubes and has gotten two different answers!

In Clip 64, Lilly and Melissa have organized their cubes into groups of ten, using two colors, brown and green. Melissa counts the cubes three different times and in three different ways.

What prompts her to count three times? The answer to this may initially elude participants since it requires them to focus on some very subtle details in the clip. The following questions can be used to help participants think about what is happening in this clip:

- What prompts Melissa's initial counting of the cubes?
- After Melissa counts each group of ten to 10, Lilly says, "so it's 30." How

- What are Melissa's different strategies for counting the cubes? Can you imitate her counting actions and words? Does she pause in her count or emphasize certain numbers? If so, which ones?
- What do Melissa's counting strategies reveal about her thinking?

Melissa begins counting after Lilly inquires, "Are you sure it's 10?" She counts each group of ten to 10 (1, 2, 3 . . . *10*, 1, 2, 3 . . . *10*, 1 2, 3 . . . *10*). After Melissa's count, Lilly says, "So it is 30." Melissa then skip counts the multilinks by tens, touching the tenth cube in each group as she counts, "10, 20, 30." She rechecks the cubes one more time, counting by ones ("1, 2 . . . 9, *10*, 11 . . . 19, *20*, 21 . . . 29, *30*), but even in this count, her emphasis, both physical and verbal, is on the decade in each group of ten.

Marking and Unitizing. In the series of clips in *Strips for the Art Show: Measurements* only Alexander and Haley (Clip 63) have a grouping strategy that is not initially indicated by *how they organize their cubes* (i.e., having a color pattern that reflects their grouping strategy). Initially, Haley's strategy is difficult to understand because his thinking is reflected not in his organization of the cubes, but in his *acting* on the materials. *How* Haley counts *is* his organizational strategy.

Haley's counting strategy—he has a finger that counts and a finger that marks the groups—is very difficult for participants to discern. Because his strategy is so complex, participants often focus on Alexander, who writes on a clipboard as Haley counts, and can be heard keeping track of the groups of ten. This is sometimes interpreted by participants as *one child is doing the counting and the other is doing the thinking*.

To help participants distinguish the layers of meaning in this clip, it might be helpful in a beginning discussion with them to focus *only* on Haley's strategy. Once they can imitate Haley's actions and pinpoint how his marking strategy changes (in the beginning, his marking finger touches each group of five; it shifts after twenty to marking a group of ten), they can begin to think about what his actions mean. Since this is, after all, *his* strategy, his thinking is reflected in his actions. What do his actions tell us about his thoughts? He marks fives and tens in his count because these groupings are important to the way he is thinking. That ten is an important unit for him becomes obvious in the second segment of the clip where he clearly marks groups of ten with a different color cube. The pink cube Haley and Alexander place to mark each group of ten is a model of *unitizing*—that ten things (cubes) can also be one thing (one group of ten), a big idea on the landscape of learning for early number.

Strips for the Art Show: Marking the Measurements

◎ *The second-grade students now mark their measurements on a strip of paper. They discuss where each mark goes on the strip. Compare the thinking of the students in the different clips. What mathematical ideas are at play here?*

The clips in *Strips for the Art Show: Measurements* show student pairs in Hildy's classroom obtaining measurements for different-sized paper. Their counting strategies for getting these measurements range from counting by ones to counting by tens.

After the children's explorations, Hildy Martin, the teacher, brings them together to build a blueprint of these measurements on a strip of paper. The clips in *Marking the Measurements* focus on student strategies for placing the measurements they have obtained onto this blueprint. Hildy supports their thinking with a repeating pattern of white and green multilinks cubes that are organized in groups of five, but she constricts their actions—the cubes are placed high up on the board and thus cannot be manipulated by the students. This constraint stretches students in a number of important ways:

- The cubes are structured in alternating groups of five (five white, five green), which can be subitized. This moves students to use these groups in their counting strategies;

- The string of cubes grouped in fives acts as a scaffold for those students counting by ones to support development toward the use of fives and tens; and

- As they build the blueprint (e.g., putting their measurements on the paper strip), students can begin to work with the numbers already placed on the paper strip. In this way, they are both using and constructing a network of key number relationships (and the idea of number space), the foundation of which is the development of a system of tens.

There are four clips in *Marking the Measurements*. Clips 66, 67, and 68 show three student strategies for placing measurements on the paper strip. All three students are using the five structure of the multilink string to help them place their numbers.

In Clip 66, Emily places 14, saying, "The white and the green and, out of the other white, just mark four." She uses the five structure to count, but locates 14 inside 15 by indicating it is one less. Underlying her strategy is the big idea of *hierarchical inclusion:* 14 is nested inside 15; it is one less.

Amirah, in Clip 67, is shown figuring out where 22 should go. She gives her answer quickly, saying, "Those two [*unitizing* two groups of ten] would be 20, and another two makes 22 [add the 2 to the 20]." Hildy slows down Amirah's explanation for two reasons: to make her strategy clearer for her classmates; and to use this strategy to highlight the system of tens she is developing.

As she re-explains her thinking, Amirah says, "white and green is 10 and that other white and green is 10 and then one, two." Hildy still pushes Amirah to be clearer in her explanation, telling her that she understands that the two groups of five are 10, and another two groups of five are also 10, but is unclear as to how that got her to 20. Amirah says, *ten plus ten equals twenty, right?* Through her emphasis on clarity, Hildy stresses that 22 is made up of two groups of ten [10 and 10 is 20] and two more.

Similar to Amirah, Josué, in Clip 68, is thinking in groups of ten. In his first explanation of where to place 35, he tells Hildy, "Take three jumps of ten." When questioned by Hildy as to where those jumps are in relationship to the multilinks string, he explains that the jumps of ten are comprised of five and five ("Put the five and five together and you're at 10 . . . and a five and a five again and that's 20 . . . and a five and a five again and that's 30 . . . and you just jump five more.") Hildy uses his explanation to place 30 on the blueprint.

In Clip 71, the question, "Where would 66 go?" (in relationship to 46 and 84), opens the door to other kinds of strategies, ones that are connected to students' development of specific number relationships. At the heart of this is the idea of number space. Sixty-six is between 46 and 84; its distance between these numbers is about halfway.

This shift—students are now considering a number in relationship to two other numbers on the blueprint—is key because it opens the door for students to use strategies based on their *own* system of number relationships. The possibilities here include

- moving to the nearest ten (either counting up or counting back);

- using ten as a tool for adding (counting up from 46, 56, 66).

In Clip 71, Shannon answers the question, "Where is 66?" by modeling the number relationships he has internalized. His words *and* actions model these relationships for his classmates. He uses landmarks to locate 66 on the number line.

Shannon demonstrates the idea of ten both as a landmark in a system of number relationships *and* as a specific measurement to mark space. He is using the number line as a tool to think with.

Strips for the Art Show: Introducing Addition

◎ *Within the context of measuring papers for the art show Hildy is introducing addition. Look at each clip. What addition strategies do you see the children use?*

You may wish to collect a sampling of strategies participants would use to solve 19 + 21 before showing Clip 73. They might

- use the previous problem and see that this new problem is 20 more, so if 19 + 1 = 20, then 19 + 21 = 40;
- use the algorithm; add the units, put down 0; carry the 1 to add to 1 and 2;
- add the tens first, then add the units;
- give the unit 1 in 21 to the 19, making 20: 20 + 20 = 40.

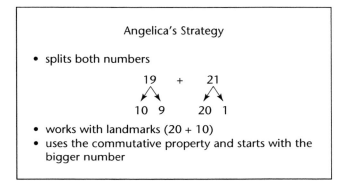

Angelica's Strategy

- splits both numbers

$$19 \quad + \quad 21$$
$$10 \quad 9 \qquad 20 \quad 1$$

- works with landmarks (20 + 10)
- uses the commutative property and starts with the bigger number

Exploring Ages: Subtraction

◎ *What ideas about subtraction are the children in Michael Galland's third grade constructing as they explore ages?*

The four clips (Clips 215, 217, 218, and 80) give participants an opportunity to think about the development of the big ideas and strategies connected to subtraction.

In Clip 215, Danny and Michelle discuss the connection between two problems: How old was my mom when I was born? and In how many years will I be as old as my mom? They use their poster to support their argument that the problems are "almost like the same, but opposite." Other students quickly pick up on this,

Danny uses this number line to answer Michael's questions about what 24 means in questions 1 and 5. It's his mother's age when he was born and how many years it will take Michael to be his mother's age. But how does this number line model both problems?

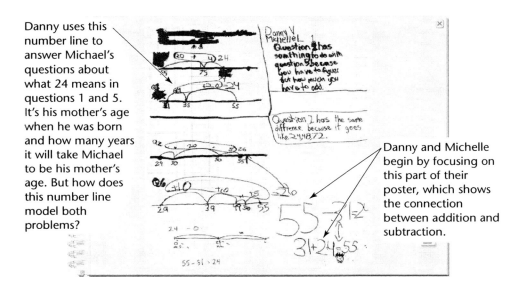

Danny and Michelle begin by focusing on this part of their poster, which shows the connection between addition and subtraction.

and comment on how the numbers are the same, but just "turned around." So while Danny and Michelle's poster *shows* that there is a connection between the two problems, how they are connected, and what the relationship is between addition and subtraction does not immediately come up for discussion because the students' comments focus primarily on the numbers themselves (e.g., they're the *same, switched around, opposite,* etc.). This connection between addition and subtraction is a big idea.

This conversation shifts when Colleen says, "Why is it doing that? Because I don't know why it's doing that and that's what's confusing me." Recognizing that the numbers are the same, but switched around, does not answer a critical question, *Why are the answers to these two different problems* (e.g., 55 – 31 = ? and 31 + ? = 55) *the same* (24)?

In Clip 217, Emmanuel and Maria's work, as evidenced in their poster, builds on the idea of subtraction as the difference between two numbers, but now moves the conversation in a new direction that supports the development of another big mathematical idea: constant difference. Their initial statement in Clip 217, "the difference was 26 . . . and these two questions that were 26, they would always talk about your mom and your brother" points to this constant relationship.

FACILITATION TIP 13

↗ One of the most important models for developing computational strategies is the *open number line,* which supports the development of some key big ideas in addition and subtraction. This model supports the development of the idea that numbers are spatially related to each other and that this relationship can be expressed as a distance on a number line. One of the big ideas that arises is the connection between addition and subtraction (24 + 31 = 55 is connected to 55 – 31 = 24). If these problems are represented on a number line, *both* solutions are contained therein.

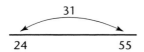

This number-line model also becomes a tool for reasoning about other fundamental relationships. One of the most important is that the distance between two numbers on a number line is constant. As students play with this model, they construct a big idea—adjusting both numbers on the number line by the same amount (this could be either by adding or subtracting) keeps the distance between the numbers the same [$x - y = (x + a) - (y + a)$]. Once students construct the idea of *constant difference,* they can play with the numbers and simplify them in ways to make the subtraction problem easier to solve mentally.

Backburner

◎ *This is the last page in the folder "Investigations." However, you may have other questions on this topic that you would like to investigate. Go to the TOOLS menu above and add them to your backburner notes.*

See *Backburner* notes, page 5.

Journey 2

In *Journey 1*—a beginning journey—participants explored the digital learning environment in its entirety. The panoply of clips on the CD-ROM offered participants a window into the development of young children's counting strategies and provided opportunities for them to think about the big ideas, strategies, and models in addition and subtraction as well.

The snapshots of children on the CD-ROM were taken from a wide range of activities that spanned early childhood—pre-K to Grade 3. These clips helped participants examine children's thinking and deepen their noticings as they engaged in kid watching.

CREATING A LANDSCAPE OF LEARNING

In *Journey 1*, participants learned how to look at students, analyzed their strategies, and probed for the mathematical meaning behind these. They also thought about the big ideas students grapple with and explored the use of mathematical models. They may even have begun to think about the connection of mathematical ideas on a landscape of learning.

In *Journey 2*, this *Landscape of Learning: Pre-K–3* CD-ROM becomes a vehicle for participants to generalize about important mathematical ideas and landmark strategies, and to ponder a number of important questions (e.g., What are the big ideas on this landscape? How do they evolve? Are some big ideas precursors to others? What big ideas and strategies are connected?).

As participants try to construct a landscape for mathematical development, they revisit the CD-ROM, selecting clips that illustrate their ideas. Whatever their arguments, the supporting evidence must be found in what children do and say on the CD-ROM. The process of reviewing the video clips with a different purpose for seeing often enables reseeing. In order to generalize (e.g., what is a landmark strategy in addition?), participants begin to synthesize their previous observations and analyses. These generalizations become the basis for constructing a landscape for mathematical development.

The Annotation Page on the CD-ROM (found under TOOLS on the menu bar) is designed to help participants organize and play with their ideas. Here they can select and clip moments from the CD-ROM that illustrate specific mathematical ideas, strategies, and models and explain the reasons behind their selections. From these annotations, they can begin to build a landscape of learning. The creation of their own landscape for mathematical development is a powerful tool that helps them reflect on student strategies and think about how mathematical ideas are connected and developed over time by learners.

LANDSCAPE OF LEARNING

Introduction

In this section you can begin the work of building a landscape of learning for early number sense, addition, and subtraction.

Clipping Moments

◉ *You can clip moments from any of the video clips in this CD-ROM. To do this, play a video clip that contains footage you would like to clip. We have provided one for you below to practice on. You can select a moment by moving the green and red sliders. To copy this clip to the clipboard, click on the clipboard icon.*

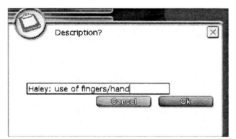

For homework, you can ask participants to practice clipping moments and creating annotations. The directions in *Clipping Moments* are clear and straightforward. However, if participants still have confusions or questions about moving the sliders and naming the clip that they send to the clipboard, these can be discussed in their small groups. Participants' own helpful hints to each other are usually effective.

Creating Annotations

◉ *Click on Annotations in the TOOLS menu. When the screen opens, you will see the clip you copied to the clipboard on the left-hand side. To make an annotation about this moment, write it where you see New Annotations. Click Next to put annotations here. To label this annotation, select from these choices: Strategy, Big Idea, or Model. If you are not sure, you can click on Undefined. To add a video, first click on the video in the clipboard section, and then click on the left arrow. To create a new annotation, click on the new page icon in the top left corner. There you can also navigate between the different annotations. Clicking on the trash can deletes an annotation.*

When participants are comfortable with *Clipping Moments* and *Creating Annotations*, they can experiment with *Pasting to the Landscape.*

Pasting to the Landscape

◎ *Click on Landscape in the TOOLS menu. You will see a graphic representation of your annotation. You can move it with your mouse anywhere you think it should be on your landscape. You can also move the landscape. To do so, click on the landscape, hold and move your mouse, or use the two bars on the right and below the landscape. On the right, you will see one or more CD-ROM icons. Clicking on the icon opens or closes the CD-ROM box and shows or hides the annotation. Double clicking on a graphic representation brings you back to the Annotation tool.*

Building a Landscape

◎ *Now revisit the footage in* Journey 1. *Clip moments where you see evidence of big ideas, strategies, and models. Make annotations for these and place them on a landscape. You will find Annotations and Landscape in the TOOLS menu. Sample dialogue is provided in Appendix D, page 58.*

Analyzing Pathways

◎ *Now that you have built a landscape, think about the placements of the landmarks. Which are related? Think about the landmarks as signposts on developmental pathways. Are some precursors to others?*

It is inevitable that, as participants begin to place big ideas or strategies on their landscape of learning, they will begin to consider (or reconsider) the relationships between them and may spend some time in thought, discussion, and debate about developmental precursors. This is part of the learning adventure and challenge to those on *Journey 2*! Sample dialogue is provided in Appendix D, page 59.

Backburner

◎ *This is the last page in the folder "Landscape of Learning." However, you may have other questions on this topic that you would like to investigate. Go to the TOOLS menu above and add them to your backburner notes.*

See *Backburner* notes, page 5.

ACTIVITY 1   **Exploring Pathways**

Once participants have built their own landscapes, have them use these as an assessment tool to think about the mathematical development of a specific child on the CD-ROM. For example, have them take their landscapes and return to *Journey 1* and revisit the clinical interview with Peter (see Appendix A). Ask them to map out Peter's journey on their landscapes. What mathematical big ideas has he developed and what strategies is he using? What are Peter's developmental pathways?

---

*Facilitators have made copies of these *Journey 2* How-To's from the Help file found under Tools on the menu bar and have given them to participants to support them on their journey.

INTERVIEW TRANSCRIPT: *SEVEN CANDIES IN A TIN*

Cathy: How old are you?

Peter: Four.

C: Four years old, oh, my! I bought something with me today in the can *(shakes the can)*. What do you think might be in there?

P: *(no response)*

C: Want to see? *(takes the lid off the can and shows him)* What is . . .

P: *(overlapping)* It's candies!

C: It's candies! Ooh, it's candies . . . wow! How many candies do you think are in there?

P: *(touches the candies in the tin as he counts)* 1, 2, 3 . . . 8.

C: You think there might be—how many?

P: *(recounts the candies in the tin)* One *(changes where he is counting in the tin and starts again)* 1, 2, 3 . . . 8.

C: So how many candies is that?

P: Eight.

C: *Eight* candies, oh, my. Let's see. *(spills the candies out on the table)* We'll put them out here. You want to check again?

P: *(as he counts, he pushes the candies away from him one at a time)* 1, 2, 3 . . . 7.

C: How many candies?

P: Seven.

C: Seven candies. Ooh. Hmm . . . you know, who are your best friends in school?

P: Herb.

C: Herb. Who else?

P: Deron.

C: And Deron. Who else?

P: Um . . . Jared.

C: Herb, Deron, and Jared. How many friends is that?

P: Um . . . four.

C: You think that's four. Let's see. Herb. Deron.

P: *(overlapping Cathy as she says the names)* 1, 2 . . .

C: . . . and Jared.

P: Three.

C: And then there's you, right? How many is that?

P: Four.

C: Four. So how many candies would I have to give if I wanted to give one to you and your three friends?

P: *(pulls over the candies, counting)* 1, 2, 3, 4.

C: That would be enough for you and your three friends?

P: *(nods his head in response)*

C: Oh, so I have enough I guess, huh? I have enough. Um . . . let's put the candies back in here for a moment *(puts the candies back in the tin)*. How many are in there? *(allows him to count the candies in the tin)*

P: 1, 2 *(stops counting)*—7.

C: Seven candies are in there. Now I'm going to put on the lid. *(puts the lid on the can and shakes it)* See, there's seven in there?

P: *(nods his head in assent)*

C: And you want to take one out for you?

P: Yes. *(takes the candy)*

C: Okay, that's yours. Now I'm going to put the lid back on. How many are in here now?

P: *(pauses to think, plays with the candy, rubs his head)* Hmm. Six.

C: You think there's six. What made you think six?

P: Um . . . *(rubs his forehead)* Because there's six candies in there.

C: Because there are six candies in there. Hmm . . . okay, you want to take another one for Jared?

P: *(nods, yes, and takes the candy out of the tin)*

C: Okay. *(closes the tin)* How many are back in here now?

P: Uh . . . five.

C: You think it's five in here now? Hmm.

P: *(nods, yes)*

C: Do you want to take one for Deron?

P: Yes. *(takes the candy out of the tin)*

C: *(closes the tin)* How many are in here now?

P: Uh . . . four.

C: You think there's four.

P: *(nods, yes)*

C: And who was your other friend?

P: Um, Jared.

C: We did Jared. We did Deron. Who else? Herb, right?

P: *(nods, yes)*

C: Herb. Do you want to take one for Herb?

P: *(nods, yes, and takes a candy from the tin)*

C: So how many are in here now?

P: Um . . . three.

C: Three. Wow. So there's three in the can and there's four *(indicates the ones on the table)* for you and your friends?

P: Yes.

C: Oh, my. And if we put them back in here and I give them to you later, how many will be in the can? Shall we do that—and I'll give those to you later?

P: *(gathers the candies and puts them in the can)* Seven.

C: Seven. Wow!

Appendix B

GAMES

CAPTURE TEN

For two players

Materials: A deck of Primary Number Cards from TERC *Investigations in Number, Data, and Space*.
A deck of number cards.

Capture Ten game board

How To Play: Two students play together.

Each turns over a playing card.

Together players try to determine the sum of the two cards and then into which pocket they should put the cards.
If the sum of the cards turned over is less than 10 (e.g., 5 and 2), players put the cards at the bottom of the deck.

For two players

Materials: A deck of Primary Number Cards from TERC *Investigations in Number, Data, and Space,* "How Many in All?"

A deck of number cards, 0–10.

Compare game board (pockets labeled 0–10) made of construction paper pockets and oaktag backing.

How To Play: Two students each turn over a card and compare them to see which is *more.*

The player whose number is more takes both cards and puts them in a pocket labeled with that higher number.

In case of a draw, the two cards are placed in the corresponding pocket.

Card play ends when all the cards have been used.

The teacher joins the players to ask what cards they think will be in the pockets she indicates.

In another version, regular playing cards can be used (the deck is 1 through 10; there is no zero, the ace is one, and all the picture cards should be removed). The game board has pockets labeled 1–10.

In yet another version, there was no game board. The teacher used paper bags numbered 0–10 (or 1–10) into which the players put their cards.

RACING DICE

For two or more players

Materials: 2 dice

Racing Dice chart (The teacher used squared paper [one-inch graph paper] for the chart in this CD-ROM.)

Magic markers

How To Play: Players, in turn, throw two dice, determine the sum, and trace over that number on a *Racing Dice* chart.

Play ends when all the squares are filled.

The play can be varied by the game board the teacher devises. In this CD-ROM version, the teacher wants the children to practice writing numerals, so she has written in all the numerals for the children to trace over.

The play can also be varied by the dice that are used. In Kathy's game, traditional dice are used. But she will probably substitute one of the dice with a die with numerals 1 through 6 on them to stretch students' counting strategies. Blank dice can be used for these variations (perhaps a die with two 4's, two 5's, two 6's) to be used with the "regular" die.

Materials: Two dice, of different colors

The Shoe Game game board

The teacher's game board for kindergartners in the CD-ROM has pairs of colored construction-paper shoes walking around an oaktag board. Because players are moving by doubles, the shoe they land on should be the second of a pair. They get a color clue if they land otherwise, and this can become the topic of a conversation about pairs or about doubles.

In one game-board version, the shoes were replicas of the shoes that the children in the class drew: sneakers, high tops, Mary Jane's, etc.

How To Play: Players, in turn, roll a die.

They make the other die match it.

Then they move their game piece that many shoes.

Play ends when the last shoe is reached.

In a variation of the play, the players can double back to Start, and the usual End is only a turning point, not a stopping point.

Appendix C

HANDY GUIDE TO THE CD-ROM CLIPS

JOURNEY 1

Folder	Page	Clips
Interviews	Seven Candies in a Tin: Peter	46
	Seven Candies: Shatisha, Sydney, and Deron	47, 48, 49, 50, 51, 98, 99, 100
	Backburner	
Routines	Attendance Chart	
	Working with the Attendance Chart	16, 17
	Attendance in Kindergarten	91
	Attendance Stick	92
	Milks in Pre-kindergarten	210, 211, 55, 96, 56
	Backburner	
Minilessons	Playing Tag	18, 19, 20, 21
	Bunk Bed Stories in Kindergarten	3, 4, 5, 6, 7
	Double-Decker Buses	93
	Arrangements on a Double-Decker Bus	8, 9, 10, 11, 12, 13, 14, 15
	43 + 20	74, 75
	192 − 40	76, 77
	Big Ideas for Subtraction	79, 83, 84, 87, 89
	Backburner	
Games	Games	
	Capture Ten	29
	Compare	28
	Racing Dice	22, 24, 25, 26, 27
	The Shoe Game in Kindergarten	1, 2
	Backburner	
Investigations	Taking Inventory: Blocks	30, 31, 42, 44, 45
	Taking Inventory: Snap Cubes	38, 39, 40, 43
	Taking Inventory: Paper Bags	34, 37
	Taking Inventory: Representing the Amounts	32, 33, 41
	Taking Inventory, Continued	36, 94, 214
	Strips for the Art Show: Measurements	57, 58, 59, 60, 63, 64, 65
	Strips for the Art Show: Marking the Measurements	66, 67, 68, 71
	Strips for the Art Show: Introducing Addition	72, 73
	Exploring Ages	215, 217, 218, 80
	Backburner	

JOURNEY 2

Folder	Page	Clips
Landscape of Learning	Introduction	
	Clipping Moments	63
	Creating Annotations	
	Pasting to the Landscape	
	Building a Landscape	
	Analyzing the Pathways	
	Backburner	

Appendix D

DIALOGUE BOXES

DIALOGUE BOX A: *SEVEN CANDIES IN A TIN*

This conversation was taken from a two-hour graduate class with in-service teachers, many of whom were first-year teachers. The participants had worked with other sections of the CD-ROM.

The facilitator paired the participants to work in small groups (these were in twos or threes) and used an LCD for whole-group discussions. The first part of their work was with the transcript from the clinical interview with Cathy and Peter. Participants were asked to look at the interview and to focus on the interaction between the child and the interviewer, and think about the kinds of questions asked, the structure of the interview, and what information the transcript gave them about Peter's mathematical development. After the transcript was examined in small groups, the facilitator brought the participants together for a whole-group discussion.

Facilitator: Who'd like to start us off? What were your observations when you read the transcript?

Participant: The interviewer started in a friendly place, by asking him a question he could answer. That made him secure—he knew his age.

P: She used candy to motivate him.

F: How did she use the candy?

P: She enticed him into participating with it—all kids like candy.

F: That's an interpretation and a generalization. Candy is part of the context in this interview. How did she use the candy, though?

P: It was a sharing situation, he was going to share it with his three friends.

P: She used it to get him to estimate.

F: Where did that happen in the interview? Remember, if you make a statement try to give supporting evidence for what you are saying.

P: When she shakes the tin and asks him, "What's in here?"

F: Help us understand how that's estimation.

P: I thought she wanted him to guess how many candies were in the tin. She asks, "What's in here?"

F: Does the question, What's in here? imply estimation?

P: What's in here? can be about what's making the noise. How many . . . I don't think she's asking that question.

P: I thought that was just to get him interested in participating—it's a mystery, ooh, what's in here?

P: She does ask the question, How many? a lot.

F: Let's focus for a few minutes on what Susan just said about the question, How many?—that question occurs often. Use your transcripts and talk in your small groups about this: I'd like you to think about two things, when does this question occur and does the question change over the course of the interview?

While small groups discuss these questions, the facilitator eavesdrops on conversations and notes certain comments made by students to highlight in the ensuing whole-group discussion.

F: Let's come together. As I was going around and listening in on conversations, I overheard some interesting points being made. Teri, why don't you share what you were saying . . .

P: Well I noticed something when we went back that I didn't the first time we looked at the transcript—her questions are really connected to what he is doing. Her questions don't come out of nowhere. It's not like she has a script.

P: My group was talking about, it's probably not the same, but I think it's related, he makes mistakes, like when he says his three friends—she asks him how many friends after he's listed them, and he says four instead of three. She doesn't say, no, you're wrong, but says, "You think that's four. Let's see . . . she re-says the names of his friends and he self corrects.

P: She's very supportive of him; she paraphrases what he says a lot.

F: How about the *How many* question?

P: She asks it a lot.

F: When does Cathy ask it?

P: Every time he counts, she asks, how many . . . ? It seems really repetitive to me. I mean he's just counted, why ask him again?

F: Interesting question. He has just counted, 1, 2, 3 . . . 8. And she says, "So how many candies is that?" Why might she be doing that?

P: Well it makes me think of something I see kids doing in my class. They count and get an answer and then for some reason, they count again.

P: Maybe they just like to count. *(laughter)*

F: Perhaps, but maybe there's something else going on here. After Peter had counted and Cathy asks, how many . . .? again, what happens? *(No response from the students)*

F: Well, let's go back to the transcript and see if we can figure it out. *(students reexamine the transcript)*

P: The first time she asks him—he has just counted the candies and gotten eight, he counts them again. After he does that she asks, how many again, and he just tells her eight. He doesn't count them.

P: But when she pours them out on the table, he counts them again.

F: So two things to consider here—the action of the interviewer, why does Cathy pour the candies out on the table? And the action of Peter, why does he recount them when she does this?

P: I think he understands when she says, "You want to check again?" that something's not quite right. He's just counted the candies in the tin twice; now she's inviting him to check. Why's she going to ask him to check if eight was the right answer?

F: So you think Cathy's emphasis is on his getting the right answer?

P: Yeah, I mean, she does it again when he miscounts his friends and says four instead of three. She says, "You think it's four." There's something about that, the way she says it, I think she's indicating to him something's not quite right.

P: It seems to me like she's supporting him, though. She validates his answers, but allows him to check them, to correct them if he needs to.

F: Why else might she want him to know the total amount of candy is seven? Any connection to what happens later on in the interview? Pablo is emphasizing that Cathy wants Peter to get the right answer, could there be another factor influencing her pouring the candies out on the table?

P: I think it's important for Peter to know there are seven candies.

F: Why?

P: The rest of the interview seems to be connected to this.

F: How so?

P: I'm not sure yet; I'll have to go back and look . . .

F: Anyone else want to comment on this? Okay, we've done a lot for our first go-around. Here's what I'd like you to do as you work in your small groups with *Seven Candies in a Tin.* For today, only look at the first interview. As you watch, I want you to focus on two things: What are Peter's strategies to solve the questions Cathy asks him? Do his strategies change? If so, how? If you find his strategies changing, see if you can pinpoint what it is that is making this happen. Remember our rules for working with a partner on the CD-ROM. Watch the clip together and take your own notes. When you're done watching the clip and taking notes, talk to your partner. See if you agree on what's happening. If you don't agree, go back and watch the clip again. Any notes you actually type on the computer, should be a consensus of the group. Remember to be specific; cite evidence for what you say about Peter, about Cathy—about anything.

DIALOGUE BOX B: *USING THE REKENREK*

The dialogue box that follows shows how a facilitator introduced participants to the *rekenrek.* It illustrates the variety of ways the arithmetic rack lends itself to individual manipulation by learners as they seek to find out *How many?* He began by asking participants to solve an addition problem. Each pair or triad of participants shared a *rekenrek* so that they could discuss and reach consensus on the strategies they decided upon.

The facilitator wrote on the board $9 + 8 = ?$ He walked around the room, observing how the participants used the *rekenrek,* and when they were finished, he began.

Facilitator: What did you get, Kathie?

Participant: 17. *(The facilitator completes the equation: $9 + 8 = 17$.)*

F: Any other answers? *(there are none).* Kathie, would you hold up your *rekenrek* so we all can see it? *(murmurs from the group that they had the same grouping)*

F: So, many of you did it like Kathie's group. Kathie, how did your group get seventeen?

P: To be honest, we just knew 9 + 8 = 17. But we pushed over 9 on the top . . .

F: Sorry to interrupt, but could you be more specific? Like, how did you move the nine beads?

P: I see what you mean. Actually we moved the 5 reds and 4 whites at once because we knew that that's 9, and then we moved 8 over the same way—in one move—on the bottom.

F: *(moves the beads on his rack according to participant's description)* And how did you know it was 17?

P: We started from 9 and then counted on the 8 beads from the bottom row: 10, 11, 12 . . . 17.

F: So Kathie's group counted on. Did any group do it another way?

P: We did. We saw the 5 + 5 reds (that's 10) plus 4 whites on the top (14) plus the 3 whites on the bottom (17).

P: Our group also saw the double-5 reds, and I guess we had doubles on our mind because when we looked at all the whites we noticed a 3 and 3 double plus one extra white bead. We moved that extra white to the side, and saw 8 + 8 for an easy 16, plus 1 is 17.

F: Slow down a bit, so we can all follow you (I can hear how excited you are). So after you noticed all the doubles, the 5 + 5 and the 3 + 3 (*he motions to these beads*) you noticed a larger double, 8 + 8 (*indicates the double*) plus an extra white for a total of 17.

P: Neat! Our group didn't do it that way, but now that I'm looking at the doubles that they did, you can do doubles another way.

F: What other way?

P: Well, if there was another white on the bottom you'd have 9 there with the 9 on the top. That's an easy double. 9 + 9 = 18. But you have only 8 on the bottom, one less than 9. So you can think of it as 18 − 1 or 17!

P: Here's another way. We made the top row 10 by moving the right white bead over to the 9 and by taking off a white bead from the 8 on the bottom. So now we had 10 + 7 or 17.

P: We knew that when all the beads are used, there are 20 all together. Three beads weren't used, so we did 20 − 3 = 17.

F: So, quite a few strategies for the same configuration: counting on, using doubles, and doubles plus 1 and minus 1, using compensation, and using subtraction! Do you have any comments about using the *rekenrek?*

P: When you asked us how to add 9 + 8, 17 is such an automatic response that I didn't think there'd be so much variety.

P: I'm glad we used the *rekenrek* because it's not like watching Brigida.

F: Say more about that.

P: Well, it's like I was so busy watching her working on her doubles that I didn't really think about the *rekenrek's* structure.

P: I think I know what Carolina means. Many of us put 9 on top and 8 on the bottom, but those red fives just popped out for our group.

So we used 10 first and added in the whites. You weren't confined to 9 and 8. Is that right, Carolina?

P: To piggyback on what Jimmy just said about not being confined, the *rekenrek* opened our group up. Physically it looks so structured, but its structure allowed us to be flexible.

F: Let's end on that profound note for today. Keep thinking about how structure allows for flexibility and continue to use your *rekenreks*.

DIALOGUE BOX C: *HOW MANY MILKS?*

One facilitator stopped the LCD right after Diane asked, "Keshawn, how many milks for sixteen children?" She wanted participants to focus on the ways Diane supports and stretches Keshawn's thinking and the kinds of questions she asks him.

Facilitator: That's an interesting question to ask three- and four-year-olds. Any comments?

Participant: I think it is way over the heads of preschool children.

P: Isn't it a no-brainer question, like Who is the George Washington Bridge named for?

P: Not for preschoolers.

F: Why do you say that?

P: Well, because I can imagine that to the four-year-olds in my class *How many milks?* would be a really hard question. I think it's too much—How many milks for sixteen children?

F: So we have some disagreement here. "It's too difficult" and "it's a no-brainer." So, I'm going to send you off with your viewing partners to watch the rest of the clips with this disagreement in mind. But before you go off, suppose I told you that Diane has made milks from cutting the face of actual school milk containers. Talk a bit with your viewing partners about how these might support Keshawn, and also think about how the structure of the attendance chart might also be supportive. Watch Clips 55 and 96 to note Keshawn's ideas and strategies, and to take particular note of Diane's questions and comments. Then watch Clip 56 to hear what Herb has to say. These are short clips, so you may be able to watch them several times before we return to talk about how many milks for sixteen children.

DIALOGUE BOX D: *TAKING INVENTORY*

The following discussion occurred in an early childhood, graduate-level course. This was the first session working with the CD-ROM, *Landscape of Learning*. As a group, the class was exploring the question, *What does a child need to know in order to answer the question, how many . . . ?* Before sending the participants off to work in pairs on *Taking Inventory*, the facilitator used Clip 30 (Noah) to develop the parameters for kid watching.

Facilitator: We're going to start our work together by looking at Clip 30 from an investigation called *Taking Inventory*, which was done in a K/1 class. The students are taking inventory of various things in the room: the blocks, the books, the multilink cubes. You will be watching a student at work in the block area—his name is Noah. For now, let's all watch it together on the LCD; later on you can go back and explore the clip more if you'd like. As you watch Noah, think about the strategy he is using and try to pinpoint exactly what happens as he uses this strategy. Be as exact as you can in your observations. After we watch the clip, we'll share our noticings.

The facilitator shows Clip 30 to the participants. After the viewing, discussion continues.

> *F:* So we've just watched Noah at work in the block area. What is his strategy? Before we start the discussion though, I'd like to set some rules . . . I'd like to go around the room and just have each person make one comment on what they saw, one thing they'd like to say about what Noah was doing. For now, I'm going to ask you not to comment on each other's ideas. Let's just put our ideas on the table. It's okay to repeat. If someone before you says what you wanted to say, say it anyway. Let's see if there is any overlapping in our noticings—or any disagreements.

> *Participant:* He was counting the blocks by ones.

> *P:* He was taking the blocks off the shelf as he counted.

> *P:* He didn't know how to count—he missed some numbers.

> *P:* He didn't seem very sure of himself. He was confused.

> *P:* I heard him miss 16, but then he continued.

> *P:* He was taking the blocks off the shelf and counting them by ones.

> *P:* It was a group effort; I heard other people talking and helping him. He probably couldn't have done it on his own, without their help.

> *P:* He missed 6, 7, and 8. I thought I heard him miss those numbers, but I'm not sure. It was hard to hear what was going on.

> *P:* He seemed to be methodical, the way he was counting (*imitates his actions of taking the blocks off the shelf*) 1, 2, 3 . . .

> *P:* His counting was purposeful. He had a reason for what he was doing. That's why he was so involved.

> *P:* He missed 15 and said 16, someone corrected him, and he went back and changed what he said.

> *P:* He seems like he needs the support of his peers—he lacks confidence in what he's doing.

> *P:* He said, "I don't know what comes after 28." He got that number from someone else—I couldn't see who it was, though. I was surprised that he didn't go back to the beginning or get confused. He just kept counting.

> *P:* He seems overwhelmed by the task—it's a lot of blocks. I think the teacher should have given him less to count.

> *P:* I agree. It's important to know your students and not frustrate them. He was obviously frustrated by what he was supposed to do—you could tell it in his body language.

> *P:* He has a name for each block he takes off the shelf, even if it's the wrong name.

The conversation continues with the facilitator writing all the responses on the LCD for the class to see.

> *F:* Would anyone like to comment on the things we've said that are similar—or different?

> *P:* A lot of people commented that he was counting the blocks by ones.

> *P:* He missed some numbers as he counted, but there were disagreements about which numbers he missed.

F: Anyone else? Okay, we're going to rewatch the clip, but before we do, I'd like to set some boundaries, to make our watching more focused. Let's try and keep our observations to what is actually said and done by Noah. Think about: What are Noah's actions? What are his words? Let's put aside interpreting his behavior. Saying things like he lacks confidence or he's overwhelmed, those are interpretations, and for right now, I'd like us to leave those kinds of noticings behind. Some of you might have questions as you rewatch it. You *(to a participant)* said you weren't sure which numbers he missed, so you might focus on that. Did he miss 6, 7, and 8? If not, which numbers, if any, did he miss?

The group views Clip 30 for a second time, after which discussion begins again.

F: Let's open up the discussion now. Feel free to make a comment or comment on something someone else says . . .

P: I change what I said. He didn't miss 6, 7, and 8. He missed 15 and said 16. I thought I heard someone counting with him, but I'm still not sure.

P: He counts the blocks by ones, but there's something I still find surprising—he keeps going from what he's counted when he doesn't know the name.

F: What would you have expected?

P: I don't know . . . it seems pretty hard to do, hold on to that number and go back to it without getting confused.

P: Yeah, in my class, kids always go back to one. I was surprised that he didn't do that. I mean they've counted the thing, they recount it, and then they'll count it again. It's like they don't remember they've just counted it.

F: That's an interesting point that we'll come back to in our discussion—What does a child need to know in order to answer the question, How many . . . ? Why do some students recount the objects they've just counted and not know—to use your words, *remember they've just counted it.* Is it about memory or is there something else at play here?

P: This time I noticed how organized he is. I mean the first time I didn't really see it—he takes the blocks carefully off the shelf, there's a rhythm to what he's doing, the action and words are together.

F: We've touched on some interesting points in our observations of Noah. He has a name for every object counted—even if it's the wrong name. Someone expressed surprise that he can continue counting or change his count and not get confused. What makes a child able to hold onto a number like that and count on from it? What ideas has he constructed mathematically to be able to do that? We're not going to answer these questions right now, but keep them in mind as you explore other children at work. Here's how I'd like you to work with your partner. Watch a video clip together, take your own notes. Talk to your partner about what you see. Remember to try—and I know this is hard—to keep your observations to the student's actions and words and avoid interpreting those actions and words. See if you and your partner agree on what it is you're seeing. If you don't agree, go back and rewatch the clip. Look for evidence from the clip to support what you are saying. When you agree, type your answers to the questions on the space provided for you on the CD-ROM.

The following conversation was taken from work done with elementary school teacher leaders of mathematics in an urban school district. In their initial work with the *Landscape of Learning* CD-ROM, the teacher leaders had explored the clips connected to the development of early counting strategies. They looked specifically at the clinical interviews as a tool for assessing student thinking in early number and the role of daily routines and games. Later in the year, they explored the development of addition and subtraction strategies. Their final work together was to build a *landscape of learning for early number*.

Prior to the conversation shown below, the teacher leaders had worked in pairs and triads analyzing the clips on the CD-ROM, writing annotations, and beginning to create a landscape of learning for mathematical development. In this whole-group discussion, the facilitator has reconvened the teacher leaders to share and post their ideas on a *landscape of learning* that is being created via an LCD with the entire group.

Facilitator: Who'd like to start us off?

Participant: We put hierarchical inclusion, the way numbers are nested inside each other—as a really important idea—early on—that kids need to know. We found several clips we thought illustrated this idea, [for example] in *Playing Tag*, when Willie splits the 4 and 3 into 3 and 3 and 1. We thought that his strategy, the big idea he was using was the nesting of numbers. We also thought clips . . .

F: Let's just stay focused on this clip for right now. *(records* nesting *as a big idea on the landscape they are building)* Comments or questions for this group?

P: We saw Willie's strategy as doubles plus one, he says, "3 plus 3 plus 1." So we put that as a big idea *and* a strategy. We didn't think of it as the *nesting of numbers*. Where's that?

P: We looked at it as the way he used the dot pattern. One of the threes in the quick image is clear; it's what kids know from dice. The other one, he pulls the 3 out of the 4.

F: *(draws the 3 and 4 die pattern on chart paper)* So this 3 he *sees* . . .

P: He subitizes that 3.

P: Doesn't he subitize the 4, too?

P: Sure, but the point is he manipulates it, splits it apart to create a fact he knows. He can only pull 3 out of 4 if he knows it's there—inside it—to begin with.

P: We used this clip to label the landscape with doubles—a fact he knows—3 plus 3 is 6. But we also thought Willie used a *counting on* strategy. He says "6, 7." So we put it on the landscape as two strategies: doubles plus one *and* counting on.

F: So is doubles plus one also a counting on strategy? What do people think?

P: He did count 3 and 3 and then one more, so he did count on.

P: I think he said "plus one," didn't he—I don't know, I could be wrong.

F: You could be right, too. *(laughter)*

F: *(continues)* Let's watch the clip one more time together, to make sure it's fresh in everyone's mind. When it's done playing, I'd like you to talk in your small groups and think about: doubles plus one. What big ideas do children have to construct to use this strategy? Is

        Willie counting on or adding on? Is there a difference between these two strategies? If so, what?

They view Clip 18 together and then, as the teacher leaders discuss the clip in their small groups, the facilitator *listens in* on their conversations. This is an important pedagogical tool not only for hearing the range of comments, but also for knowing which group to use to start the discussion.

> F: Let's come back together. *(looks at participant)* Why don't you start us off.

> P: The problem he was solving was 3 plus 4. He says that. "That's 4; that's 3." But his strategy is to look inside the 4 and pull out a number that was inside. So we think doubles plus one has to be connected to hierarchical inclusion. You can't use that strategy without splitting numbers into the double you want to use and what's left over—putting it back in.

> P: We agree with that—nesting—for doubles plus one, but we were wondering what does it mean to count on? Did Willie know 3 and 3 *plus* one, or did he know that 3 plus 3 equals 6 and that the next number is 7? So, is he counting on, or adding one?

> P: Well we were thinking that maybe with *one more*, how can we really tell if the strategy is counting on or just adding?

> F: Can you give us an example of what you mean?

> P: It would be clearer with 2; 6 plus 2 equals 8, that's adding up. If it were a counting on strategy, he would say, "6, 7, 8."

> F: So how are these strategies similar? Different?

> P: Both of them, keep 6 whole and add 2 to it.

> F: What big idea underlies keeping 6 whole?

> P: Cardinality.

> F: So how are these strategies different?

> P: Counting on isn't as sophisticated.

> F: Why not?

> P: The adding up strategy would be connected to what Willie actually says, it's *plus 1*—in this case, *plus 2*. It seems somehow—and I'm not totally sure of this—connected to two parts coming together to make a whole. The counting on strategy, I don't see the two groups coming together to make a new group.

> F: So now let's place these on our landscape. Where shall we place them? Discuss these questions in your working group for a few minutes. Then find some more clips and label and paste them.

DIALOGUE BOX F: *ARE SOME BIG IDEAS PRECURSORS TO OTHERS?*

The following conversations were taken from a discussion on the *Landscape of Learning*. Students had created their own landscapes and shared them in small-group discussions. In a whole-group discussion, the facilitator worked to stretch participants' thinking about the relationships of big ideas and strategies on the landscape by using one they had previously built.

> *Participant:* Our group disagreed about where we placed certain things on our landscapes—we pretty much had the same big ideas and strategies, but we put them in different places.

Facilitator: Does it matter that people place things in different places?

P: Well I think, yes—I think it does. We were having this big discussion around compensation. We all had it as a strategy, but some of us placed it lower on the landscape than others.

F: I'd like us to think about, what does it mean to place something *lower* on the landscape.

P: Maybe I'm confused about this, but I thought that the way we build our landscape should show the connection between big ideas and strategies.

F: So how are strategies and big ideas connected? Are some precursors to others?

P: Yes. That's what we were talking about with compensation.

F: So the question you were thinking about was where does this go on the landscape? I'd like everyone to think about this for a few minutes in your small groups. When we come back together, I'd like to hear several arguments for where this should be placed.

P: Before we go off to work, I have a couple of questions that came up in our group. If the landscape is a metaphor for development, would each child have a different horizon?

F: Nice question. *(to the group)* What do you think?

P: I think if you're assessing a child, you can use it as a tool to help you—I mean if we think of Peter in the interview *Seven Candies in a Tin*, his horizon is different than Shatisha's. But you can also use the landscape as a model for learning so that it's general.

F: So when it's used as a general model for mathematical development, where would you place compensation? What are connecting ideas? Are there some ideas that are precursors to others? We'll come back in a few moments and discuss this together.

As participants discuss compensation, the facilitator listens to conversations and chooses which group will begin the whole-group share.

F: Rick, why don't you start us off?

P: We thought compensation was connected to part-whole relations, which is a big idea. In order to use compensation as a strategy a student would have to be able to decompose numbers into parts.

P: We agree, but we had another big idea that connects to this and that was cardinality. A student wouldn't break a number into parts if he wasn't able to think of that number as a whole. And cardinality is early in development.

F: *(moves cardinality and part-whole relationships lower on the landscape as big ideas)* So where should we place these on our landscape in relationship to compensation?

P: Cardinality is one of the big landmarks, but it's pretty early on in development. So I'd place it lower on the landscape near one-to-one correspondence. But part-whole relations has to be further along moving toward the horizon.

F: Why is that?

P: Because we've seen children who have had cardinality—Deron—in the clinical interview, but he hadn't developed part-whole relationships. I remember that clearly. He could count to seven, knew when he was asked, *How many is that?* that he had seven, but when he had the candy in parts—five in the tin and two on the table—he didn't know how many there were altogether. He didn't conserve the total amount.

F: So I also hear you saying that connected to part-whole relations is another idea: conservation.

P: Yes, I think conservation should go up there as a precursor to compensation.

F: We've begun to build a landscape now that is different than the ways many of you designed yours. What I'd like you to do for homework is take the original landscape you made and now begin to think about how ideas and strategies are connected. Think about where you place things as developmental pathways, so that if a child uses a certain strategy think about what big ideas must have been constructed for that strategy to be used.